Subject Analysis:
Computer Implications of Rigorous Definition

by
Jessica Lee Harris

With a preface by
Maurice F. Tauber & Theodore C. Hines

The Scarecrow Press, Inc.
Metuchen, N.J.   1970

Z
695
.H27

Acknowledgments

Without the aid and encouragement of several organizations and a number of individuals this study could never have been performed.

Professors Maurice F. Tauber and Theodore C. Hines gave freely of their time, effort, and ideas; saw to it that the required support would be available; and most importantly, made clear at several crucial points their conviction that the study could be successfully completed. Professor Alice Bryan helped throughout with problems of research methodology. Other members of the faculty of the School of Library Service, Columbia University, gave much useful advice when it was needed.

The Bro-Dart Company, and Mr. David Remington in particular, provided financial support, access to files available nowhere else, and clerical help. Messrs. William Welsh and Richard Angell, together with others at the Library of Congress, freely gave advice and suggestions, and permitted the author access to the official catalog and shelf-list and other files at the Library.

The U.S. Office of Education provided a research grant which covered a good deal of the expenses of production of the dissertation, while the School of Library Service provided a Title II-B fellowship and other financial support.

The Columbia Computer Center and its personnel, under the direction of Dr. Kenneth King, coped cheerfully when the author arrived, totally innocent of any knowledge of computing, with a problem different in nature from any they had dealt with in the past. In particular, Mr. Pete Kaiser simultaneously helped with the problem and educated the author.

Finally, the author's husband contributed from beginning to end by cheerfully enduring all the inconveniences and dislocations which seemed to be unavoidable in study for the doctorate.

Table of Contents

Manual Styling; Editing after First Sort; Summary

List of Tables

Table   Page

14. Miscellaneous Form Headings   139

15. Piano Music Headings   169

16. Number of Occurrences of each Style Change   173

17. Number of Styling Errors, by Major Types
     of Change, Found in Pre-Keypunching Edit   174

18. Styling Changes, Grouped by the Ability of
     the Computer to make them   180

19. Analysis of Hyphenated Compound Words   183

20. Headings made Ambiguous or Awkward by
     Styling Procedure: Inverted Prepositional
     Phrases   188

21. Headings made Ambiguous or Awkward by
     Styling Procedure: Other Forms   190

22. Headings and Cross References which would
     File Together by Styling Procedure   192

23. See and See Also References from Direct to
     Inverted Heading Forms   204

24. Cross References to Terms used as Sub-
     divisions Under Place Names   206

25. Cross References from Terms in Parentheses   210

26. Headings Containing and   213

viii

Preface

Subject analysis for information retrieval is an area which always seems deceptively simple to those without previous background in it, however extensive their background in specific subject disciplines may be. The basic requirement seems easy enough: to structure the statement of a subject in such a way that it can be placed into, and retrieved from, an ordered file.

While attempts have been made to use simple, non-complex terms or even single words, it always becomes evident that single words are often insufficient to express a subject, and that some subjects are in themselves complex. To express such subjects requires either that their constituent concepts--not words--be separated and then recombined, or that only one part of the subject be shown.

The former solution requires that the indexer perform the necessary analysis and synthesis, and then separate the constituents for the searcher to reassemble. The latter forces the seeker of information to sort through many items to find those bearing on the complex topic he wants, and may require the indexer to decide under which part(s) of the concept an entry should be made.

It is probably fair to say that all systems for subject analysis, whether computer-based or completely manual, evolve in the direction of greater complexity of terms. Surprisingly, there has been little study of existing long-established complex systems of subject analysis used with

9

large universes to determine which of the complexities of such systems may serve a useful purpose and which may simply represent the accretions of age or unevaluated precedent.

Dr. Harris' work represents such a study. It is both interesting and instructive that the Library of Congress subject headings, which were her primary experimental universe, constitute what is probably the most complex and fully-developed structure for alphabetical subject analysis in existence today. In a way, this fact may be construed as a balm to librarianship, but its connection with librarianship, often unjustly thought to represent only the past of information science, seems to have acted as a psychological barrier to its examination by both theoretical workers in information science and those practitioners in the field who design tools and compile thesauri.

The emphasis in this study is on those aspects of this complex subject analysis structure which seem most likely to cause problems in the attempt to use subject headings in computer systems. That this is an area of current practical as well as theoretical importance can be seen in the kind of limitations on terms set by the joint Engineers Joint Council-Project Lex rules and conventions for compilation of thesauri, which include a limit (36 characters) on the length of terms and on the punctuation which may appear in terms (parentheses, and in rare cases, hyphens, only are allowed).

Dr. Harris has identified a number of these aspects which might cause problems, setting as her second goal as rigorous a definition of the current manual procedures as possible. These definitions, in turn, made it possible to make judgments about the value and use of given structural characteristics of the headings. In many cases, she has then been able to suggest alternatives to them which preserve or augment their value while making the structure pattern sufficiently distinctive and rigorous to permit their use in computer systems.

This procedure of attacking problems of subject analysis steers quite neatly, it seems to us, between the more customary Scylla of ignoring the accumulated and tested experience of the past, and the Charybdis of attempting to mechanize an existing system as it stands, including all its errors and all those aspects of it which were geared around a different technology.

On the purely practical level, conversion of existing library subject catalogs and heading lists to machine-manipulable form (the term is not synonymous with machine-readable, as many discover to their dismay) is a very present problem. Dr. Harris' work involved devising a set of procedures for clerical revision of the form of subject headings which, with professional editing, will permit them to be computer-arranged in a useful order without requiring explicit coding or the punching of sort keys.

It has been a very productive working hypothesis at the Columbia University School of Library Service that developing the implicit theoretical basis underlying large, pragmatically developed information systems leads to highly productive new insights. We would consider Dr. Harris' work a major substantiation of this hypothesis.

One of the most interesting aspects of her study, for example, is substantiation and explication of the idea that the Library of Congress subject heading list is much more than the most important library list in existence. It is also an ad hoc faceted classification scheme which shows the

11

way to important theoretical advances in selective faceting. Her work here has opened a broad range of new possibilities, both for faceted classification as such, and for the improvement of library subject heading work, in making existing faceting more explicit, more consistent, and more useful, especially for computer-based systems. It opens the way, explicitly, for more economic and hence better and more frequent production of more complex vocabulary control devices by computer for all types of listings, including the Library of Congress list itself.

This is an important development in subject analysis. Its derivation in librarianship should not obscure the fact that our colleague's work represents pioneering new advances in information science.

Maurice F. Tauber
Melvil Dewey Professor of
Library Service

Theodore C. Hines
Associate Professor of
Library Service
Columbia University

Chapter I

Introduction

The need for a comprehensive code for subject heading work has long been recognized, but there has been so little research in the area of form and structure of subject headings and the subject catalog that even the first requirement of a code--definition of present practice--could not be met, except in a few areas. The state of the art has not really advanced a great deal since the publication of the first edition of Cutter's _Rules_ in 1876. Even much of what is generally thought to be true of subject headings is not backed up by evidence. It has always been known that the subject catalog was not fulfilling its functions as well as it should--whatever these functions were considered to be. The situation has become even more acute in recent years, with the simultaneous increase in publication and in library book budgets. A system that works even fairly well in a library of a given size may break down completely when the collection increases by an order of magnitude--and this rate of increase has not been unknown in recent years.

A further complicating factor is use of the computer and other mechanical devices to perform tasks which were originally built around the abilities of human beings. Many characteristics of the subject catalog are present simply because the system grew without much advance planning, and humans could deal with the results. To use a computer effectively requires at least a minimum of systematization. To use people effectively also requires systematization.

This study was undertaken to provide descriptions of present subject heading practice in certain important areas, based on a belief that it is not useful to propose new practices without determining the value of the old.

History of Subject Headings

The history of subject control of information is only slightly shorter than the history of any attempt to control or provide access to recorded information. The earliest bibliographical tools were simply inventories, more closely related to shelflists than to any other tool in use today, but it soon became customary to group these inventories in some sort of order by classes.

One form of bibliographic classification, however, is only about a century old. The alphabetical subject heading uses as its classes the most arbitrary ones conceivable-- the letters of the alphabet. Codified by C. A. Cutter in 1876,[1] it probably derives from two predecessors: the alphabetical indexes which classification schemes required as soon as they became at all involved, and catchword title entries which were used at least by the nineteenth century to provide subject access to the contents of books and journal articles. Title words were early recognized to be inadequate as a means of subject access, largely because of the problems of synonymy and nonindicative titles.

Arrangement of subjects directly by the letters in the words used to describe them, rather than according to any other possible order (e.g., a hierarchical classification), means that a person who knows the name of his subject can go directly to it in the file. Hierarchical classification is mainly of use for survey of a whole area, or for

browsing. Demand for many years has been increasingly
for the specific item of information rather than for an over-
view of a broad area.[2] A major factor in this increasingly
specific demand, of course, is the fact that more knowledge
than ever before exists on any given subject. The result
has been the evolution of alphabetical subject headings.

It is important to realize that subject headings are
essentially a phenomenon of the United States. In other
countries, until the last few decades, when subject access
was provided at all it was by means of such devices as the
classed catalog (in Great Britain) or the Schlagwort, or
catchword title, catalog (in Germany). Since World War II,
however, the alphabetical subject catalog seems to have been
receiving more acceptance in Europe.

The sole exception to this rule is the Vatican Library,
which invited a group of librarians from the United States to
devise a new catalog for the library. The result was the
Vatican Norme.[3] The Norme included a long section on
subject cataloging. This section followed Library of Congress practice to a large extent, but was much more extensive and clearer than anything available in English. Until
the English translation of the second edition was published
in 1948,[4] the best codification of alphabetico-specific subject heading practice was available only in the Italian language. The third edition of the Norme was translated into
French and published in 1950;[5] a comparison of this edition
with the English translation of the second edition has shown
that there has been no significant change in the subject heading rules between the second and third editions of the Norme.

Alphabetico-specific subject headings, as known today,
are largely the result of the work of one person--Charles

Ammi Cutter. His rules for subject cataloging have never
been superseded.[6] In fact they have really only been modified slightly and extended in the ninety years of practice
since they were first published. And it would probably be
possible to make a good case for a claim that many of the
modifications have not been improvements, but the reverse.

At any rate, Cutter's rules were made before the
literature explosion had begun to reach the dimensions it
has today. The minute topics on which journal articles and
even books are produced now were hardly conceivable then.
In addition, Cutter was obviously not sure himself about
certain important points, such as the possible limits beyond
which specificity[7] ought not to go. This uncertainty has not
diminished with the passage of time. Cutter's famous remark (occasioned by the rise of the Library of Congress
card), in the "Preface" to the fourth edition of his Rules,
"Still I cannot help thinking that the golden age of cataloging
is over, and that the difficulties and discussions which have
furnished an innocent pleasure to so many will interest them
no more,"[8] was certainly mistaken. There has been a
great deal of standardization--on the desirability of this
standardization there can hardly be said to be complete
unity[9]--but important problems remain for the subject cataloger, whether or not he tries to follow the Library of Congress.

In 1911, J. Kaiser published his Systematic Indexing.[10] Although his system was designed for office files, it
could have had considerable influence on library subject
heading theory. Apparently developed independently of
Cutter,[11] Kaiser's concrete, country, and process were a
logical extension of the principle of specific entry. Kaiser,

for the sake of consistency, would have indexed under the
name of things, adding as subhead whatever was done to the
thing. He even went so far as to turn Bibliography into
Books (concrete) - Description (process). He got around
the problem of whether to enter under subject or place by
entering under both. Only processes were never entry
terms (unless treated in general terms, rather than in relation to a given material or thing).

Kaiser's system went too far for most librarians
(although Prévost's noun rule is related);[12] he never mentions the principle of reader usage. However, his distinction between concrete and process, or thing and action,
sheds considerable light on what Cutter was probably searching for in the principle of specific entry. Unfortunately, for
a variety of reasons Kaiser's work has never received the
attention it deserves; his book is now almost unobtainable.

When the Library of Congress decided on the dictionary form for its catalog and began to publish its catalog
cards around the turn of the century, the form of the subject catalog in the United States was determined. Whether
or not the form of alphabetical subject catalog actually produced by the Library of Congress decision and its practice
since then is, all factors considered, the most desirable, is
impossible to say. [13] No other form has ever received a
really fair trial, but by the early 1940's it was evident that
the subject catalog was not living up to expectations. [14]

An important theme in the literature for several decades has been the need for principles of subject analysis,
or for a body of theory, or for a code of practice. None
of this has been forthcoming. Prévost attempted to cut the
knot with the noun rule. [15] She would have largely abolished

usage as a criterion for selecting subject terms. Instead,
entry would always be under the "thing" as subject, with
specificity achieved by the subhead. Even the forms of
words would often be changed by this method. For instance,
International Relations would become Nations - Inter-rela-
tions. Although she stated that this system had been used
successfully for some years at the Newark (New Jersey)
Public Library Business Branch, there is no record of its
ever having been applied elsewhere.

In 1947, Julia Pettee's Subject Headings was published. [16] As an historical account it is interesting and useful, although somewhat sketchy. Despite the subtitle, there
is very little theory in the book; Miss Pettee was too occu-
pied, as was Haykin later, with the need to arrange inherited
practice into a system with some meaning.

David J. Haykin was engaged in codification of subject headings at the time of his death in 1958. The only
available information on his projected code is an outline of
general topics he planned to cover. [17] His Subject Headings:
A Practical Guide[18] is neither theoretical nor a code. It
was intended to satisfy two needs:

> First, the recurrent necessity at the Library of
> Congress of providing trainees in subject catalog-
> ing with the rationale and basic rules of practice
> in the choice and use of subject headings; and,
> secondly, a necessary basis of common under-
> standing of subject headings for libraries partici-
> pating in cooperative cataloging. [19]

Progress toward a comprehensive code for subject headings
remains at roughly the same stage as at the time of Haykin's
death.

Metcalfe has advocated the dictionary catalog against
some of its competitors, and in the process has contributed

in several areas to elaboration of subject heading theory.[20]

Recent developments in classification and indexing theory, often related to machine applications, may in the future have some effect on subject headings. The theory of facet analysis, of which Ranganathan was the first major exponent, makes explicit and compulsory one feature which has been present but has been implicit and optional in subject headings. Likewise, a process analogous to chain indexing procedure may be found in the practice of downward subject heading see also references. The contribution of chain indexing and facet analysis is largely limited to theoretical proposals by the proponents of these systems--usually without adequate understanding of the purpose and contribution of alphabetico-specific subject headings to information control. If facet analysis, chain indexing, and other techniques were fully applied to subject headings, the end result would be a different kind of subject analysis--and much study is needed to determine if the change would be beneficial.

Coordinate indexing, and the numerous thesauri which have been developed using the principle of coordination, represent another form of subject analysis with implications for subject heading theory. Many subject headings are "precoordinated," i.e., two or more substantively separable concepts are listed sequentially, to form a heading progressively limiting the scope of the heading to achieve increasing narrowness of meaning. An example is:

Woman - Diseases - Diagnosis

which combines two independent concepts: "women" and "diseases," plus a third, "diagnosis," that by itself is susceptible to a much wider range of meaningful associations. However, an implicit basis for the formulation of subject headings according to accepted systems is diametrically opposed to the assumptions underlying coordinate indexing. Thus, in the construction or selection of actual subject headings, the term to be utilized for searching purposes is regarded as complete in itself; in coordinate indexing two or more terms are searched and only those documents fulfilling some specified condition of presence or absence of each term are selected for retrieval. In this and other respects in which newer systems and theories of subject analysis directly affect construction of subject headings, they are discussed more fully in the following section.

Review of the Literature

Because Frarey's review covers the literature of subject headings to 1959 very thoroughly,[21] the present discussion, as it relates to materials published before that date, is intended to be selective rather than comprehensive in scope.

Purpose and function of the subject catalog

Any study of factors influencing formation and choice of subject headings must be designed and conducted within the context of the purposes and functions that the subject catalog is intended to fulfill. Two traditional functions, however, appear to be in conflict, namely, those of survey and of selective identification. Little systematic study has been made of the relative effectiveness of the subject catalog in fulfilling these functions. What little evidence exists seems to indicate: (1) that because of its inherent structural basis the alphabetical subject catalog does not satisfactorily provide comprehensive survey; and (2) that attempts to modify its structure toward meeting this pragmatic criterion of utility

may hinder effective fulfillment of the function of selective
identification.

> Since definition of function rests ultimately upon a
> knowledge of need, an assessment of limitations,
> and an awareness of status or place within a uni-
> verse of information systems, and since our com-
> prehension of each of these matters is still far
> from precise, it is clear that whatever amorphous
> body of theory, conception of purpose, or defini-
> tion of function underlies our practice is little
> more than tradition or folklore at best. [22]

It seems evident that very little verifiable knowledge
is available as yet on which to base a definitive judgment
as to the possible multiple functions the subject catalog can
and must fulfill if it is to satisfy all proposed, but non-
conflicting, criteria of utility as a bibliographic tool. However, there is a consensus that the basic function of the
subject catalog is to provide specific information needed by
the non-specialist in a particular field. It is within this
necessarily limited conceptual frame that the present study
has been undertaken.

Use of the subject catalog

Although the methods of investigating use made of the
subject catalog are much in need of improvement, there is
sufficient similarity in the results of these studies to justify
certain conclusions, for example, that workers resort to the
subject catalog primarily for study outside their special
fields.

Principles of subject headings

The two main principles on which subject heading
work is based are little changed since Cutter enunciated
them in 1876. They are specificity and usage.

Specificity

Cutter's first rule for subject headings was: "Enter

a work under its subject heading, not under the heading of
a class which includes that subject."[23] He then used three-
quarters of a page of fine print in a note on the problem of
determining the subject in certain kinds of cases. Subjects
with "no name," but described only by an indefinite phrase,
for instance, would have to receive class entry. Furthermore, "it is not always easy to decide what is a distinct
subject." For instance, is <u>Extempore preaching</u> sufficiently
distinct to warrant a heading separate from <u>Preaching</u>?

 Nowhere in his rules does Cutter define specific entry explicitly enough to show whether he thought of it as
including the aspect or point of view from which a subject
is treated. However, in his <u>Rules</u> and in most of the literature on subject analysis since, there is an implicit assumption that specific entry includes the aspect or point of
view from which a subject is treated.

 One of the major problems of the principle of specific
entry is the amorphousness of the concept as it is usually
used. Lilley has shown that specificity is determined by:

1. Subject area (minuteness of the topic desired).

2. Particular library (the example for this
characteristic shows that Lilley means the
degree to which subdivision by aspect or
point of view is used).

3. Particular book (for some books, analytics
might be preferable to the broader heading
covering the entire item).

4. Searcher's need at a given moment.

5. A chance relation between the user's momen-
tary need and a book the library happens to
own.[24]

 Specificity in subject headings, as a concept, is
probably useful only in conjunction with the concept of liter-

ary warrant--that is, no concept, regardless of how important it is, will appear as a subject heading in the catalog
unless literature on the concept is represented in the subject
catalog (and for practical purposes in most libraries, this
means whole books on the concept).

However, even when literary warrant is used as a
criterion, the standard subject heading lists often refer from
more specific headings for which there is certainly literary
warrant to more general headings. The Sears list refers
from Seaweeds to Algae.[25] McDonald has shown that there
are numerous concepts in the humanities for which the standard lists do not provide subject headings.[26] One of his examples is that of Ghost towns. Material on this subject in a
library using the Library of Congress list[27] was entered at
the time under Cities, Ruined, extinct, etc. It is interesting
to note that in the new seventh edition of the Library of Congress list,[28] Ghost towns has finally achieved the status of
a see reference to Cities, Ruined, extinct, etc. But entry
is still not specific!

In the Wilson indexes, new topics are listed under
more general, established headings until the newer terminology can be verified.[29]

Other limitations on specificity are adopted as general
policies. In Readers' Guide, names of some kinds of individual things are entered under the name of the class. For
instance, the Queen Mary was entered under Steamships and
steamboats; specific racehorses were entered under the general topic. For specific movies, there is not even a see
reference from the name of the picture.[30] In Readers' Guide
today the situation has not changed significantly. Inspection
of recent volumes shows that specific ships are entered under

Ocean liners with reference from the name of the ship.
Racehorses are entered under Horse racing or Horses without reference; movies under Moving-picture plays, variously
subdivided.

Van Hoesen proposed entering materials under the
general subject in preference to the specific one when the
latter has so little material "that the reader would have to
look under general too."[31] He seems not to consider the
possibility that it might be precisely those topics for which
sorting through the entries under a general heading will produce few references that should be brought out under their
specific names.

Sharp has suggested a return to the alphabetico-
classed[32] principle in some areas, based on "common
sense."[33] However, the general applicability of common
sense as a pragmatic solution to this type of problem is not
clearly inferrable from the few examples he gives. Specificity is possible with the alphabetico-classed arrangement;
it is simply indirect. (Here, too, is another cloudy area.
When specific entry is discussed, it sometimes seems that
directly specific entry is being implied. In other words, is
it justifiable to speak of specific subject headings and alphabetico-classed subject headings as if the two concepts
were antonyms?)

The Sears list of subject headings intentionally does
not attempt to achieve full specificity. The editor states
this policy as follows:

> A common criticism of any list concerns the de-
> gree of specificity in its headings. Specificity is
> relative and depends on the size of a library, its
> functions, and its patrons. In a small collection,
> the use of too specific headings can result in
> scattering like materials. Practicality rather

than theory should determine the degree of
specificity. [34]

Jackson has compared the Sears and Library of Congress (LC) headings by examining the headings applied to
the same books in two of the Wilson catalogs and in the National Union Catalog. [35]   He found that the headings were
identical in 40 percent of the cases.   In slightly over one-
fourth of the cases remaining, the differences were not due
to greater specificity in the LC headings.   This means that
in approximately 45 percent of the cases he examined, according to Jackson's concept of specificity, as inferred from
the definition given in his article, the Sears heading is less
specific than the LC heading.   Although he divides the differences into categories, it is not possible to determine
what proportion of these cases fall into each category.   For
instance, Jackson's data does not indicate how often the
Sears heading actually represents a more general class of
objects than the LC heading, and how often it simply re-
flects LC's freer use of aspect and form subdivisions.

In LC subject heading practice, which is the basis of
practice in most American libraries, there have been many
attempts to compromise between a dictionary and an alphabetico-classed catalog by such means as inverted subject
headings, combination of subject words, and subordination of
subjects to each other. [36]

The Library of Congress also has used catchword
title entry[37] for topics for which no subject heading has
been established.   In fact, a number of anomalous practices
seem to be largely due to reluctance to establish a new
heading for a new topic.

Metcalfe, in his several books, has given what may

be the best available exposition on the problem of specificity, and points to a possible solution.[38] His proposal is
that specification be absolute so far as the object of study
is concerned, and that specification of the aspect or point of
view from which the object is studied be limited by desirability and needs of the library or the topic.

Furthermore, so far as specification of very narrow
topics is concerned, he proposes a principle that might be
usable.   This principle is that entry be specific so long as
the name of the smaller subject does not include the name
of the larger; and that where the name of the larger is included, either class or inverted entry might be used.   For
example, Siamese cats might be entered under either Cats
or Cats, Siamese.

Part of Lilley's dissertation involved the specificity
of the subject headings used in the field of English literature.[39]   However, he was not particularly concerned with
the specificity of the headings as applied to books, but rather
with the broadness or narrowness of the topic described by
the heading.

In MeSH (Medical Subject Headings)[40] some rather
interesting departures from conventional subject heading
practice were used.   The list was based on the older subject
heading list used by the National Library of Medicine but
was revised to become a part of MEDLARS (Medical Literature Analysis and Retrieval System).   The headings in MeSH
are designed for machine coordination.   (For example, a
journal article on osteomyelitis of the femur will receive
the headings Osteomyelitis and Femur.   When material on
this topic is requested, both words must be used as search
terms.   The rationale is that by this method it is also

possible, if desired, to retrieve everything in the system
on the Femur and everything on Osteomyelitis.

Despite its title, MeSH is not a subject heading list
in the normal sense; it is a thesaurus. In a subject heading list, far more terms are included by implication than
actually appear in the list. Species, place, personal and
corporate names are important examples of kinds of terms
which are used as subject headings but appear in the list
only as examples. Typically, vocabulary control in a thesaurus is rigid; only terms actually listed in the thesaurus
are acceptable in the system. A subject heading list functions as a guide to form of terms and to the referencing
structure, and as a record of decisions as to which of two
or more synonymous terms to use.

In one study the entries under a group of ten MeSH
headings, which in the January, 1963 issue of Index Medicus
had more than twenty entries each, were counted in the
issues of Index Medicus for the next six months. In this
period, these headings accumulated from 270 to 700 entries.
The conclusion of the study was that while the MeSH list
may work well for machine searching, it is not adequate for
manual use, since large numbers of entries may accumulate
under headings very quickly. While it is theoretically
possible (although inconvenient) to coordinate entries manually, the study also showed that some items entered under
Liver (which accumulated 700 entries in six months) were
entered only there. [41]

Rogers' paper in the Institute on Subject Analysis of
Library Materials is an excellent indication of the thinking
which led to MeSH. [42] He gave as an example an item on
treatment of Osteomyelitis of the Femur with Streptomycin,

which, according to him, would require three headings. He
makes no mention of the possibility of subdivision in some
arbitrary but useful order (e.g., some medical lists, depending on the main area of interest, always subordinate a
part of the body to a disease affecting it).

Rogers also stated that some scientific terms were
too specific. For instance, the National Library of Medicine
had received over 2,000 books in the field of bacteriology
published over the past thirty years, less than 100 of which
discussed a given genus or species. His solution to this
problem was a decision to use only genus names except
where there was a good deal of material on the species.
Here is an instance where the concept of literary warrant
would certainly have been useful. Almost certainly, the
areas in which books are published about a single genus or
species of bacteria are precisely the areas in which workers
would be interested in books about the particular genus or
species. To require these workers to sort through a long
undifferentiated file for the material they need--and to rely
on the title to indicate the subject of the book--is certainly
not an adequate answer to the problem.

When MeSH was being revised for its second edition,
some of the problems encountered in manual use were taken
into consideration. As noted above, a large number of headings had accumulated an unmanageable number of entries.
It would seem from her article that Sewell may not fully
have realized the magnitude of this problem. It is necessary
to put together numbers from two separate pages of this
article to discover that nearly 25 percent of the headings
used in MeSH accumulated over 100 articles in two years of
the Cumulative Index Medicus. On pages 167-168, she

states: "...for a large proportion of the material in the
1960 and 1961 issues of Cumulative Index Medicus, no further subdivision seemed really necessary.   Only about 1,000
headings attracted as many as 100 articles." On page 169,
we are given the figures for total number of headings in
MeSH--4,400 in the 1960 edition; 5,700 in the 1963 edition.[43]

The problem is not confined to difficulty in manual
searching of a tool designed primarily for machine use. In
the original edition of MeSH it was not possible by any means
to search for articles on a particular virus.   All viruses
were entered, both in the machine and in the printed lists,
under six groups only.   In the second edition of MeSH this
was increased to forty-three groups.[44]

It would appear that the makers of MeSH had abandoned specificity, even in its narrowest definition (specificity of the object of study, not necessarily of the point of
view from which studied) as a principle of subject analysis.
However, the needs for both specificity and subdivision of
major topics seem to be gradually becoming recognized.   In
the 1966 edition of MeSH several hundred new main headings,
and about seventy topical and form subdivisions, were added;
in the 1967 edition there were 200 new main headings and
eleven new subdivisions.   There is every indication that the
list will continue to grow.[45]

There has been one study comparing LC subject headings with MeSH subject headings.[46] Yale Medical Library
compared the LC-type headings used by Yale with the MeSH
headings for 515 books with a 1962 imprint (Yale did use a
few headings more specific than those in the LC list).   For
slightly over three-fourths of the books, all LC subject headings could be matched by equivalent headings in MeSH, if

MeSH headings which would require coordination were included.   For somewhat less than one-fourth of the books,
there was at least one subject heading applied by LC that
could not be matched in specificity by MeSH headings. Many
of these included headings that appeared in MeSH only as
see references to more general headings.   In LC there was
a total of 101 subject headings, used a total of 136 times,
that were not matched in MeSH--15.8 percent of the total
number of subjects.   And the LC list is a general list, although Yale Medical had used some additional headings for
medical topics.   In addition, a conservative estimate indicates that 987 MeSH headings were required to match 863
LC-Yale headings.   The authors concluded that MeSH is an
adequate tool.

Direct entry

        Closely related to the concept of specificity, at least
in American practice, is that of direct entry.   In fact, in
discussions of specific entry it is often evident that directly-
specific entry is being assumed.   However, it is possible
to achieve specificity via subheading, as Sharp has proposed. [47]

        One of the most interesting and far-reaching depar-
tures from conventional practice is the "noun rule" proposed
by Marie-Louise Prévost. [48] So far as is known, the concept of the noun rule originated with Schwartz, who used it
in his catalog of the New York Apprentices' Library, and
recommended its use to Cutter.   It has not been possible to
find any published discussion of the noun rule before
Prévost's 1946 article.   Her principle is that "All headings
begin with the noun indicating the subject."   In the case of
subjects usually described by an adjectival phrase, the noun

is placed first as the entry word, followed by the adjective
changed to the noun form as a subdivision using the dash.
In effect, specificity is achieved by means of subdivision,
not by direct entry. Prévost's use of the noun rule has
other implications, discussed below under Usage.

The Air University Library in its Periodical Index
has, on the contrary, carried the principle of direct entry
beyond conventional practice.[49] In part, this is an instance
of the special requirements of a subject-specialized collection. In corporate names, especially those beginning with
U.S., hierarchical entries have been dropped; entry is under
the name of the subordinate body, whether author or subject.
In addition, certain other subdivided entries are reversed.
U.S. Air Force - Chaplains has become Chaplains - Air
Force. Furthermore, phrases are used instead of subdivisions in numerous cases. Thus, parts of airplanes are entered as phrases beginning with the word Airplane instead of
as subdivisions under Airplanes; for example, Airplane fuselages instead of Airplanes - Fuselages.

Usage

Cutter's prefatory statement as to choice between
different names for subjects is: "General rules, always
applicable, for the choice of names of subjects can no more
be given than rules without exception in grammar. Usage
in both cases is the supreme arbiter--the usage, in the
present case, not of the cataloger but of the public in speaking of subjects."[50] In the area of English literature, at
least, LC main headings do generally follow usage as shown
in the titles of books.[51]

It is necessary to distinguish between usage of terms
as words and grammatical usage in the English language.

It is generally accepted that subject headings have their own
grammar and syntax which depart from the usual grammar
and syntax of English language (e. g. , inverted adjectival
headings, subdivisions). While it is certainly valid to question the need for some of the usual deviations from conventional grammar and syntax in subject headings, this is really
a separate problem from the matter of choice of words. The
latter is the subject of discussion in this section.

There are many examples of failure to follow the
principle of usage in the LC list of subject headings. Cookery is a pertinent example, but there are others.

The principle of usage and that of specific entry are
often believed to come into conflict. Knapp has shown that
users do not understand the principle of specific entry. [52]
They will often look under the name of the including class
on one of two assumptions: that the library could not possibly
have a book on a topic as small as that of, say, camels; or
that all the books on camels will be entered not only under
Camels but also under Animals.

Even beginning library school students, who presum-
ably would, if anything, have greater knowledge of libraries
than average, do not understand specific entry. Lilley analyzed the subject headings suggested by beginning library
school students for finding other books like six named in a
test question. The 340 respondents suggested 373 different
subject headings for the six test titles. There were from
forty-one to ninety-two different headings for each title. The
analysis showed that, of errors in specificity, terminology
and form, almost half of the suggested headings were incorrect in all three ways. Most significantly, lack of an understanding of specificity was a factor in 93. 4 percent of the

incorrect headings. [53]

Thus, whether or not usage in the sense of how readers approach the catalog is accepted as a principle of subject analysis, it is necessary to be certain that users receive adequate instruction and cross referencing to guide them through the catalog. What these studies and others like them have actually tested is not usage in the normal sense--that is, in writing about the subject or speaking of it in conversation--but rather the special usage of readers searching the catalog. The only real test that has been made of the former type is Lilley's on book titles in the area of English literature, and he found that subject headings did correspond to usage.

Usage in either sense is not uniformly accepted. Prévost's method rejects it almost entirely. [54] Her idea is that a uniform and comprehensible, even if arbitrary, rule that can be explained to users is preferable to the unavoidable inconsistency involved in the rules (or lack of them) usually followed. The noun rule, as proposed by Prévost, would turn Intercultural relations into Cultures - Interrelations.

It is probably justifiable to say that almost any form of subject analysis using alphabetical arrangement of terms must be guided at least partly by usage. The words selected for use must be drawn from some source. In the example above (Cultures - Interrelations), the transformed heading is derived from a phrase suggested by usage. The transformed heading, however, requires the patron to go through an extra mental step. If users now cannot (or do not try to) grasp filing arrangements and entry rules, it seems highly unlikely that they will have much more success in an attempt to

transform such an expression as <u>Intercultural relations</u> into
the form selected by the cataloger.   Such transformations
as <u>Relations - Intercultural</u> or <u>Relations - (between) Cultures</u>
are just as conceivable.

    This last possible heading brings up another point.
In the case of headings which require a prepositional phrase
to show the relation between two terms connected by the
dash, Prévost would enclose the preposition in parentheses
to show that it is ignored in filing.   Thus another complica-
tion is introduced.   In addition, her examples show that the
word(s) enclosed in parentheses are not actually ignored in
filing.   Rather a mental inversion is performed on the heading so that if two or more subject headings are identical except for the part enclosed in parentheses, they are sub-
arranged by the terms in parentheses.   Thus, <u>World War,</u>
<u>1939-45 - Peace - (affected by) Democracy</u> is placed before
<u>World War, 1939-45 - Peace - (effect on) Democracy.</u>

Form of subject headings

    Subject headings have been produced in a variety of
forms that is, to say the least, bewildering.   They include
adjectival phrases, inverted and uninverted; nouns connected
by prepositions or conjunctions; single words, singular or
plural; series of terms separated by a comma.   Two or
more of these forms may occur in combination in the same
heading; any may be followed by a defining term enclosed in
parentheses; they are all capable of being subdivided by use
of the dash--or once again a combination of these complexities may occur.   Daily has studied the form of the headings
in the LC list and compiled an exhaustive listing of those
that occur, together with their combinations. [55]   He has
shown that the choice of heading form, once the words which

best express the subject have been chosen, is largely
governed by the requirement to fit the heading into the existing heading structure. In other words, he produces con-
vincing evidence that the usual course of events is for the
cataloger to decide where the new heading should appear
(between which two older headings, or in which subgroup),
and then word the heading in such a way that that is where
it files.

Lilley, in his study of subject headings drawn from
several subject heading lists in the area of English literature, used a "sentence formula." Briefly, he devised from
the subject heading a sentence "describing the kind of material the heading seems intended to represent." He then
applied the criteria of this formula to the sentence to derive
a heading, and compared the derived heading with the original one. While he proposed no universal validity for his
formula, he did show that, in general, headings (except, in-
terestingly enough, those used by the New York Public Library) derived by the sentence formula are practically
identical with the original heading. In addition, those headings which did not match the sentence formula are generally
those which are questionable on other grounds. The reason
for the failure of the NYPL headings to match the sentence
formula seems to be NYPL's greater use of alphabetico-
classed arrangements until very recent times. [56]

LC subject headings are inconsistent in form. The
evidence presented by Daily of ad hoc decisions, rather than
use of a consistent policy, shows the basic reason for this
inconsistency.

A separate problem from inconsistency in form is
the evidence presented by Frarey as a result of his study

of LC subject heading revision from 1941 to 1950. [57] He
found that the emphasis of subject cataloging was shifting to
use of common terms, in preference to "cataloger's choice"
headings. He felt that this shift was the cause of the grow-
ing complexity of headings--more parenthetical expressions,
more topics treated in relation to each other, and more
phrase and hybrid headings. The reason he cites for the
shift may be valid, but its usefulness is questionable. Certainly Cookery (Apples) never appeared on a title page or in
conversation. The more different kinds of headings, each
sub-arranged in its own little group, which appear under a
given entry word, the more complicated it is to find a given
heading, even when the terms in which it is expressed are
known.

Geographical headings

When a topic is treated in terms of a country or
geographical area, the problem arises of which to use as
entry word--topic or geographical term. There is no satisfactory answer to this question. Cutter recognized that the
only completely satisfactory way is to make double entry,
under both subject and country. However, since this practice would increase the bulk of the catalog, he recommended
entry under country as a general rule, subdivided by topic,
on the grounds that entry under topic subdivided by country
would lead to alphabetico-classed arrangement. His recommendation has not been followed but the reasons for the
choice in most cases are hard to find.

One attempt has been made to determine if choice in
the LC list between entry under place and entry under topic
is correlated with the LC class to which the heading may be
assigned. [58] Except in a very few classes (law being one of

them) no consistent pattern was found.

Summary: The State of the Subject Heading Art

If this study were of the state of research in subject headings, it would have to conclude that it is almost non-existent. There are scientific studies of particular areas but these illuminate only a small part of the broader problem. However, when pragmatic experience over a period of several generations is added, our knowledge of the problem is considerably greater.

The state of the art is this: the subject catalog serves a variety of purposes, inadequately defined and sometimes conflicting. There is, however, a general consensus that it serves best the person inquiring outside his own narrow special field, or in a new field. The attempt has been to make the subject catalog serve the conflicting purposes of generic survey and specific reference, even though the need for the former has been inadequately demonstrated.

There are two basic principles of subject heading work: direct-specific entry, and usage. These likewise are sometimes in conflict and neither has been consistently followed. Beyond these principles there is a broad area for which they provide little or no guidance, and in which practice is painfully inconsistent.

Form of subject headings is based almost entirely on pragmatic considerations, not on a consistent theory. In addition, forms have become more complex in recent years.

Louise Darling has put the situation aptly:

> ...we have come to the conclusion that most of our agonizings, ponderings, and disquisitions on how to organize subject display in the catalog for the greatest convenience of the reader are superfluous. A logical, orderly plan for development of the subject catalog is not an idea of any real

substance to the average reader. If he is cornered
in discussion, he will admit that there has to be
some system to follow, but he doesn't much care
what it is if it is simple and will lead to the book
he wants quickly. He has only the vaguest notion
of the need for organization that must go into the
catalog. He gets what he wants from the subject
catalog more often than not. To be sure, he
would like to hit the subject jackpot every time,
but he is not actively dissatisfied with things as
they are...He would probably even be willing to
agree with our head cataloger that, though the
subject catalog requires continual updating and revision, after all it cannot be designed for morons.[59]

Factors in Formation and Choice of Subject Headings

This assertion, that the subject catalog cannot be designed for morons, takes another fact for granted; that is,
that the subject catalog is by its nature a result of some
design. This is not to say that the factors in the design
have been entirely consistent, consciously applied, or correct by any standard, but simply that some design is always
used. A design, or structure, is essential if the purpose of
the subject catalog, aid in retrieval of stored knowledge by
subject, is to be fulfilled.

The purpose of this study is to determine the effect
of certain factors on formation and choice of subject headings. Assumptions basic to the study are that:

1. Subject access to materials provides a useful
   form of bibliographic control.

2. Some form of access similar to the alphabetico-
   specific subject heading will continue to be
   useful and used.

3. Once the entry term has been selected, the
   grammatical structure adopted for the terms
   of a heading is largely determined by the need
   to find the best possible location in the existing structure for the new heading.

4. Usage of terms in English language is a
major factor in selection of the terms of a
subject heading.

Very few of the factors in formation and choice of
subject headings have been adequately investigated. The
factors chosen for study were of three types: (1) those
affecting the formation of new subject headings to fit the
existing structure; (2) those affecting application of existing
subject headings to actual books; and (3) those involving the
structure of the subject catalog as a whole.

The factors in the first area are:

1. The influence of the number of titles entered
under a given subject, or of a large body of
literature on a special aspect of the subject,
on the introduction of aspect subdivisions.

2. The influence of a felt need for classified sub-
arrangements, or of a preference to enter
under the term best specifying the subject,
on the form of entry of adjectival phrases.

The factors in the second area are:

1. The influence of the nature, size, or objectives of the library collections for which cataloging is designed on the choice of subject
headings for application to the same books.

2. The influence of the size of the file that would
accumulate under the heading on application of
form headings and headings denoting the type,
rather than the subject, of a work.

The factors in the third area are:

1. The need for changes in styling of subject
headings to make possible a consistent and
useful arrangement by computer--and a corresponding need for rationalization of existing
complexities of subject heading form and filing.

2. The possibility of adoption of a general policy
for establishment of cross references from
components of headings other than the one
chosen for entry.

Certain other assumptions and limitations were made
which affected formulation of the hypotheses and the
methodology by which they were tested. The study was
limited to subject cataloging for collections of general subject scope, because specialized collections offer special
problems. In general, only subject headings applied to
monographic works were used because the minute subjects
of such forms as periodical articles would also open a whole
separate area of problems.

The object of the study was to determine the influence
of the factors involved as broadly as possible. Since the
cataloging done by the Library of Congress has more influence than any other source in the United States today, its
subject heading list and catalogs were used throughout the
study, with the addition of Wilson cataloging when cataloging
intended for different types of libraries was being compared.
Since current practice is the issue, the latest available edition (seventh except where otherwise specified) of the Library
of Congress subject headings was used.

With these limitations, hypotheses covering the factors under consideration were formulated as follows:

A.   Two major factors in introduction of aspect sub-
     divisions of specific subjects are:

     1.   Avoidance of long files under a given heading.

     2.   The need to bring out the existence of a signifi-
          cant number of books on a given aspect of the
          subject, even when the size of the total file
          under the subject is not particularly large.

B.   Use of inverted adjective-noun combinations, in
     preference to:

     1.   Direct entry of these combinations is dependent
          on which of the two words may be regarded as
          best specifying the subject.

    2.   Subdivision by means of the dash, is used to
achieve a classified subarrangement by use of
punctuation marks (for example, <u>Cookery</u>,
<u>American</u> could be written as <u>Cookery - Ameri-
ca</u>, if it were preferred to arrange it in the
same file as <u>Cookery - History</u>).

C. Choice of the subject heading proper (exclusive of
aspect subdivision) for application to the same books
is not dependent on the nature, size, or objectives
of the general library collections for which subject
cataloging is designed.

D. Application of form headings and headings denoting
the type (e.g., <u>Fiction</u> as a heading for novels)
rather than the subject of a work is significantly
correlated with the size of the file that has accumulated or would accumulate under the heading (i.e.,
in open stack libraries form headings are used only
when there are or would be a small number of entries under the form).

E. Styling of subject headings can be effected in such
a way as to make feasible a consistent and meaningful computer arrangement, using (for arrangement) only the characters appearing in the entry.

F. In cases permitting the adoption of a uniform policy
for establishment of cross references (for example,
from the direct to the inverted form of heading
when the latter has been used), no consistent policy
has been followed in the LC list.

Expected Significance of the Study

The study was planned for the contribution it could make
in two major areas: (1) elucidation of the basis of present subject heading practice to aid in the formulation of a much-needed
subject heading code; and (2) to help provide a basis for the ad-
justments which will be essential if major catalogs are to be
computer-produced in a satisfactory manner. Its implications
go beyond these goals, however, to include contributions to subject heading theory and to practice in special areas such as book
and periodical indexing and subject-specialized collections.

Notes

1. C. A. Cutter, Rules for a Printed Dictionary Catalogue.

2. Julia Pettee, Subject Headings; the History and Theory of the Alphabetical Subject Approach to Books.

3. Vatican Library, Norme per il Catalogo degli Stampati.

4. Vatican Library, Rules for the Catalog of Printed Books, trans. from the 2d Italian ed. by T. J. Shanahan, et al.; ed. by W. E. Wright.

5. Vatican Library, Règles pour le catalogue des imprimés, edition Française. Cité du Vatican, Bibliothèque Apostolique Vaticanne, 1950; [Texte établi sur la troisième edition italienne.]

6. Cutter, Rules, p. 37-48.

7. The terms "specific entry" and "specificity" have never been precisely defined. In this chapter, which is primarily a review of the literature, in each case the term must be assumed to have whatever meaning the author cited assumed for it. Where precise definition is required, the best possible interpretation of the author's intended meaning will be given. In later chapters the terms will be avoided, and more precise substitutes used. It is illuminating that the term used to denote the base principle of subject headings has never been precisely defined.

8. Cutter, Rules, 4th ed., p. 5.

9. Oliver Linton Lilley, "Terminology, Form, Specificity, and the Syndetic Structure of Subject Headings for English Literature, " p. 26-27.

10. J. Kaiser, Systematic Indexing, n. p.

11. John W. Metcalfe, Information Indexing and Subject Cataloging, p. 235.

12. Marie-Louise Prévost, "Approach to Theory and Method in General Subject Heading, " Library Quarterly, XVI (April, 1946), 140-151.

13. Lilley, "Terminology, Form, Specificity," p. 26-27.

14. Andrew D. Osborn, The Crisis in Cataloging.

15. Prévost, "Approach to Theory and Method."

16. Pettee, Subject Headings.

17. David J. Haykin, "Project for a Subject Heading Code."

18. David J. Haykin, Subject Headings: A Practical Guide.

19. Ibid., p. v.

20. Metcalfe, Information Indexing.

21. Carlyle J. Frarey, Subject Headings, Vol. I, Part 2.

22. Ibid., p. 56.

23. Cutter, Rules, 4th ed., p. 66.

24. Oliver Linton Lilley, "How Specific is 'Specific?'"
    Journal of Cataloging and Classification, XI (January,
    1955), 3-8.

25. Minnie E. Sears, List of Subject Headings, 9th ed.,
    p. 533.

26. Gerald D. McDonald, "Application and Limitations of
    Subject Headings; Humanities," in Subject Analysis of
    Library Materials, ed. by Maurice F. Tauber,
    p. 55-63.

27. U. S. Library of Congress, Subject Headings used in
    the Dictionary Catalogs of the Library of Congress,
    ed. by Marguerite V. Quattlebaum, 6th ed.

28. Ibid., 7th ed.

29. Sarita Robinson, "Problems in the Production of Subject
    Indexes," in Tauber, p. 204-209.

30. Ibid.

31. H. B. Van Hoesen, "Perspective in Cataloging with some
    Applications," Library Quarterly, XIV (April, 1944),
    100-107.

32. The alphabetico-classed catalog had a few representa-
     tives in this country early in this century, but it is
     not used now. In it the general topics are arranged
     alphabetically, with the smaller topics they include as
     subdivisions under them. For instance, in the al-
     phabetico-classed catalog a book on dogs would be
     entered under Animals - Dogs; one on terriers would
     be under Animals - Dogs - Terriers.

33. Henry A. Sharp, "Cataloguing: Some New Approaches.
     5. The Dictionary Subject Approach," Library
     World, LVII (December, 1955), 92-94.

34. Sears, Subject Headings, p. 6.

35. Sidney L. Jackson, "Sears and Library of Congress
     Lists of Subject Headings, Report of a Sample Com-
     parison," Illinois Libraries, XLIV (November, 1962),
     608-630.

36. John W. Cronin, "The National Union and Library of
     Congress Catalogs: Problems and Prospects,"
     Library Quarterly, XXXIV (January, 1964), 77-96.

37. "Catchword title entry" is, essentially, entry under any
     word in a title except the first word not an article.

38. John W. Metcalfe, Information Indexing; Alphabetical
     Subject Indication of Information, Rutgers Series on
     Systems for the Intellectual Organization of Informa-
     tion, Vol. III; Subject Classifying and Indexing of
     Libraries and Literature.

39. Lilley, "Terminology, Form, Specificity."

40. U. S. National Library of Medicine, "Medical Subject
     Headings," Index Medicus, VI, No. 1, Part 2
     (January, 1965).

41. Eleanor Haydock, "MeSH List and Book Cataloging in
     Medical Libraries," Medical Library Association
     Bulletin, LII (July, 1964), 545-556.

42. Frank B. Rogers, "Application and Limitations of Sub-
     ject Headings: the Pure and Applied Sciences," in
     Tauber, p. 73-82.

43. Winifred Sewell, "Medical Subject Headings in
     MEDLARS," Medical Library Association Bulletin,
     LII (January, 1964), 164-70.

44. Ibid.

45. Frank B. Rogers, "Problems of Medical Subject Cata-
     loging," Bulletin of the Medical Library Association,
     LVI (October, 1968), 355-364.

46. Benedict Brooks and Frederick G. Kilgour, "Compari-
     son of Library of Congress Subject Headings and
     Medical Subject Headings," Medical Library Associa-
     tion Bulletin, LII (April, 1964), 414-419.

47. Sharp, "Cataloguing."

48. Prévost, "Approach to Theory and Method."

49. Oliver T. Field, "An Application of the Direct Entry
     Principle to Indexing," American Documentation, VII
     (July, 1956), 225-228.

50. Cutter, Rules, 4th ed., p. 69.

51. Lilley, "Terminology, Form, Specificity."

52. Patricia B. Knapp, "Subject Catalog in the College Li-
     brary: an Investigation of Terminology," Library
     Quarterly, XIV (July, 1944), 214-228.

53. Oliver Lilley, "Evaluation of the Subject Catalog:
     Criticisms and a Proposal," American Documentation,
     V (April, 1954), 41-60.

54. Prévost, "Approach to Theory and Method."

55. Jay E. Daily, "The Grammar of Subject Headings: A
     Formulation of Rules for Subject Headings based on a
     Syntactical and Morphological Analysis of the Library
     of Congress List."

56. Lilley, "Terminology, Form, Specificity," p. 49-50.

57. Carlyle J. Frarey, "Subject Heading Revision by the
     Library of Congress, 1941-1950."

58. Bartol Brinkler, "Geographical Approach to Materials
     in the Library of Congress Subject Headings," Li-
     brary Resources and Technical Services, VI (Winter,
     1962), 49-64.

59. Louise Darling, "Readers' Impressions of the Subject
     Catalog," Medical Library Association Bulletin,
     XLIX (January, 1961), 58-62.

Chapter II

Use of Aspect Subdivisions

By far the most common complex subject heading
form is the subdivision set off from a main heading by a
dash. Unlike other complex forms, dashed subdivisions may
be added to any heading. Subdivisions may serve the same
purpose as any other form of modifier;[1] in addition, certain
needs are rarely or never met by any other heading form.
Haykin distinguishes subdivision from qualification, "in that
it [subdivision] is ordinarily used not to limit the scope of
the subject matter as such, but to provide for its arrangement in the catalog by the form which the subject matter of
the book takes, or the limits of time and place set for the
subject matter."[2] The discussion which follows, however,
makes it clear that the use of subdivisions extends far beyond these limits. Haykin distinguishes four major types of
subdivision:[3] form (Agriculture - Abstracts; Agriculture -
Congresses); local or geographic (Education - France); period
or time (U.S. - History - Revolution; Germany - History -
1517-1648; Aeronautics - Early works to 1900);[4] and topical.
The last is essentially a catch-all for all subdivisions not
included within the first three groups.

According to Haykin, subdivision may be used, "if
the number of works on the subject is large, of if the subject matter is presented from a special point of view or to
serve a special purpose, or is limited with respect to the
time or place covered or the type of facts presented."[5] It

47

appears that most subdivisions are applied on an ad hoc
basis, dependent largely on the cataloger's perception of a
need to break down the file of entries under a heading into
more manageable segments.

Subdivisions Excluded from the Study

a)   Form subdivisions

A major exception to this ad hoc approach is form
subdivisions. Haykin's discussion implies that whenever a
work is in a particular special form the heading is always
subdivided by that form.[6]

Form subdivisions describe the way in which a topic
is treated, i. e., in general a form subdivision means not
that a particular part of the topic is treated or that the topic
is treated from a special point of view, but rather that the
topic is treated as a whole by means of this special device--
a dictionary, a laboratory manual, etc. Since a number of
terms often called form subdivisions do not fit this defini-
tion--History, for example--it is well to be as precise as
possible. For purposes of this discussion, the term form
subdivision refers to form of publication or literary form.
History and criticism, Laws and legislation, and similar
subdivisions were not treated as form subdivisions in this
study. Haykin lists generally applicable form subdivisions.[7]
Below are listed: (1) the terms considered form subdivisions
for the purposes of this study, with an asterisk following
those which also appear in Haykin's listing; (2) the terms in
Haykin's listing which were not treated as form subdivisions
in this study; and (3) other terms which might be questionable, but were not treated as form subdivisions in this study.

1. Terms treated as form subdivisions in this study:

Abbreviations
Abbreviations of titles
Abstracts
Addresses, essays,
  lectures*
Analytical guides
Anecdotes, facetiae,
  satire, etc.
Bibliography*
Bio-bibliography*
Biography
Catalogs
Catalogs and collections
Catechisms and creeds
Charts, diagrams, etc.
Chrestomathies and
  readers
Classification
Collected works*
Collections*
(Collections)
Congresses*
Conversation and phrase
  books
Conversation and phrase
  books (for soldiers, etc.)
Correspondence, reminis-
  cences, etc.
Curiosa and miscellany
Diagrams, tables, etc.
Dictionaries*
Dictionaries and encyclo-
  pedias
Directories*
Discography
Drama
Drawings
Examinations
Examinations, questions,
  etc.
Facsimiles
Film catalogs
Fingering charts
Forms, blanks, etc.

Gazetteers
Glossaries, vocabularies, etc.
Handbooks, manuals, etc.*
Hymns
Illustrations
Juvenile films
Juvenile literature
Laboratory manuals
Lantern slides
Legends
Legends and stories
Lists of vessels
Manuscripts
Maps
Maps, Outline and base
Maps, Pictorial
Maps, Topographical
Meditations
Miscellanea
Non-commissioned officers'
  handbooks
Officers' handbooks
Orchestral studies
Outlines
Outlines, syllabi, etc.*
Periodicals*
Personal narratives
Photographs
Pictorial works
Pictures, illustrations, etc.
Poetry
Portraits
Prayer-books and devotions
Problems, exercises, etc.
Programmed instruction
Quotations, maxims, etc.
Rates and tables
Readers ([subject])
Regimental histories
Registers
Regulations
Relief models
Reproductions, facsimiles,
  etc.

Road maps
Scores [all subdivisions
  of music headings con-
  taining this word]
Seamen's handbooks
(Selections: extracts, etc.)
Sermons
Societies*
Societies, etc.*
Songs and music
Statistics*
Statistics, Medical
Statistics, Vital
Stories
Stories, plots, etc.
Sources
Studies and exercises

Studies and exercises
  (Jazz)
Tables and ready-reckoners
Tables, calculations,
  etc.
Tables, etc.
Tables, standards, etc.
Text-books for foreigners
Texts
Thematic catalogs
Translations from
  [language]
Translations into
  [language]
Yearbooks*
Zoning maps

2. Terms in Haykin's list, not treated as form subdivisions:

Exhibitions
History

Study and teaching

3. Other questionable terms, not treated as form subdivisions:

Art
Audio-visual aids
Case studies
Cases
Cases, clinical reports,
  statistics
Comparative studies
Composition and exercises
Constitutional law
Contracts and specifi-
  cations
Curricula
Doctrinal and
  controversial works
Early works to 600
Early works to 1800
Foreign words and phrases

Information services
Law[s] and legislation
Laws and regulations
Licenses
Mathematical models
Notation
Patents
Private collections
Safety regulations
Self-instruction
Specifications
Standards
Suffixes and prefixes
Surveys
Terminology
Terms and phrases

Some explanation of the decision not to treat the
terms in lists 2 and 3 as form subdivisions may be in order.
In the case of the terms in list 2, it is clear that Haykin
used the term "form subdivision" somewhat loosely. For

example, a history of a subject is not in any sense a form
of treatment; its history is one aspect of the subject. Many
if not all of the terms in list 3 can be and are used as
form subdivisions. The list was compiled empirically from
evidence of entries actually found in the LC's official catalog
that these subdivisions are at least as likely to be used for
works about the form as works in the form. In these cases
the term is better treated as an aspect subdivision. Some
of the terms in list 1 are very occasionally used for works
about the form, but the preponderance of uses in all cases
is for works in the form.

  b) Geographic subdivisions
        Geographic subdivisions are actually a special type of
aspect subdivision, applicable "when the data of the subject
treated are limited to a geographic or political area."[8]
These subdivisions are always arranged in a separate file,
and, while the decision to use geographic subdivision at all
is very likely associated with the hypothesis as it was formulated, application of the various possible geographic subdivisions should be determined solely by the existence of
literature on the subject limited to a given area. For this
reason geographic subdivisions were also excluded from the
study.

Aspect Subdivisions
        Haykin's third group of non-topical subdivisions, time
or period subdivisions, are not actually a distinct type.
While most such subdivisions are arranged in a separate
file, this is simply because their arrangement is by the
numbers in a date, implicit or explicit, and therefore by
definition outside the A to Z sequence. Furthermore, many

other kinds of subdivisions could be distinguished, some of
which are also sometimes filed separately.

All subdivisions which are neither form nor geographic were included in the study. The limits of inclusion
in the universe of topical subdivisions are determined as
much by accidents of terminology and phraseology in subject
heading as by any objective definition of parts of subjects or
points of view from which they are treated. For instance,
airplane wings are an identifiable subject, not an aspect of
the subject airplanes. Yet the term appears in the LC subject heading list as Aeroplanes - Wings, and therefore must
be treated as a topical subdivision. On the other hand, airplane stability is certainly an aspect of the subject Stability
as it pertains to airplanes. However, since the subject
heading is Stability of aeroplanes this aspect does not appear
as a topical subdivision.

A working hypothesis was adopted: that two major
factors in introduction of aspect subdivisions of subject headings are: (1) reduction of file length under a given heading;
(2) the need to make manifest a significant number of books
on a given aspect of the subject, even when the size of the
total file under the subject is not particularly large.

Reduction of File Length
In order to test the hypotheses, an 0.8 percent random sample of used main headings (311 headings) was selected from the magnetic tape of the seventh edition of the
LC subject heading list. Then these headings were checked
in the official catalog of the Library of Congress. The
number of cards under the unmodified heading, and under
each subdivision--form, topical, or geographical--was de-

termined. Furthermore, the number of cards under subdivisions (where they existed) of form and topical subdivisions
was also determined. Sub-subdivisions of geographic subdivisions were not investigated, since these files were generally quite large, and these subdivisions were not the major
focus of the study.

The cards were counted individually except where the
file under a heading or subdivision was an inch or more
long. In this case the working figure of 100 cards per inch
was used and the file was measured with a ruler. A similar procedure was used when a file of geographical subdivisions was over an inch long: it was measured, and the file
was searched to determine the number of place names
actually used. When the file was over twelve inches long, a
sample of every third or fourth inch was searched to determine approximately the number of place names involved.

When the findings were tabulated, it was discovered
that a larger sample would be necessary. There were 314
headings in the sample at the end of the test (two headings
were removed, as they were not used headings but partial
terms to which a general reference was made from another
form or spelling; while five were added as a result of expansion of inverted bracketed headings, e.g., Photographers,
Danish, [Russian, etc.] into several headings. Of these,
243 had no topical subdivisions, while 47 had only one, leaving 24 headings with from 2 to 92 topical subdivisions.

An expansion to a sample of 5 percent was decided
upon, to provide about 150 headings with two or more topical
subdivisions. The remaining 4.2 percent sample was selected at random from the LC subject heading list tape by
the same means as before. However, there was no need to

look up another 1,650 headings in the LC catalog, when
about 75 percent (those with no topical subdivisions) would
not add to the value of the sample, and another 15 percent
(those with only one subdivision) would be of minimal value
only.   The printed LC subject heading list does not include
all the subdivisions of headings which appear in the LC official catalog; however, it seemed reasonable that the headings
with numerous subdivisions in the official catalog would also
be subdivided in the heading list.   To check this hypothesis,
the seventy-one headings in the original sample which had at
least one topical subdivision in the official catalog were
searched in the heading list, with the results shown in
Table 1.   Eliminating from the second sample all those headings with no subdivisions in the heading list would eliminate
about 70 percent of the headings with one subdivision in the
official catalog, and a third of those with two or three, but
few or none of those with four or more subdivisions.

TABLE 1:   Status in LC list of headings subdivided in official
           catalog

Topical subdivisions in official catalog	Any subdivision in LC list?	
	Yes	No
1	14	33
2	3	1
3	3	2
4 or more	15	0

Observation showed that the existence of topical subdivision was correlated with that of geographical subdivision,
so the occurrence of a specification of the latter in the sub-

ject heading list was also noted. This device selected 18 of
the 243 headings--about 7.5 percent--with no topical subdivisions in the official catalog, while also selecting nine of
those with one subdivision and one of those with two or three
subdivisions. Thus, use of this device improved selection
of the single subdivision headings from 30 percent to 50 percent; and that of the two- and three-subdivision headings
from two-thirds to 75-80 percent.

Since the results of this check were satisfactory, all
the headings in the larger sample were also searched in the
LC list, and only those with subdivisions or instructions for
geographic subdivision were searched in the LC official catalog. All the headings in the earlier small sample were
also included. There were a total of 339 headings in the
sample of which the subdivisions were checked in the official
catalog. Table 2 shows the distribution of the headings by
number of subdivisions, with the mean, median, and range
of the number of unsubdivided and topically subdivided entries
per heading.

While the distribution is still highly skewed toward
the low end, there are enough headings with multiple subdivisions in the sample to permit statistical analysis. Ac-
cordingly, Pearsonian coefficients of correlation between the
number of subdivisions and the total number of unsubdivided
and topically subdivided entries per heading were calculated
for the entire sample and for several subsets of the sample.
The coefficients are shown in Table 2.

The 95 percent confidence limits were calculated by
a statistician for the coefficient of correlation of the full
sample. At this level the true coefficient falls within the
range from .611 to .731. His analysis of the data led to

TABLE 2:   Distribution of headings by number of topical
           subdivisions in official catalog

No. of subdivisions	No. of headings	Entries per heading (form & geog. subdivs. excl.)		
		mean	median	range
0	105	47	9	0-725
1	92	83	21	0-1228
2	32	130	47	3-1421
3	17	114	98	4-282
4	14	287	299	6-907
5	15	216	136	30-505
6	5	167	161	14-402
7	7	335	127	49-1558
8	8	462	201	13-1530
9	5	222	175	19-407
10	1	715		
11	3	320	418	20-522
12	3	626	740	202-936
13	4	598	529	121-1213
14	2	405	405	94-716
15	1	785		
16	1	101		
17	1	125		
18	3	422	309	288-669
19	2	401	401	104-698
21	1	176		
31	1	859		
32	1	514		
33	2	430	430	211-648
34	1	242		
43	1	2708		
47	1	215		
54	1	833		
56	2	1973	1973	1195-2751
74	1	2193		
77	1	2036		
78	1	979		
89	1	3477		
92	1	316		
95	1	1158		
149	1	1726		

Section of sample	Pearsonian coefficient of correlation
Entire sample	.675
1-149 subdivs.	.599
0-21 subdivs.	.386
0-9 subdivs.	.369

the conclusion that the lower coefficients found for the subsets of the sample were due to the greater variability of the
data in the lower portion of the distribution.

Correlation coefficients were calculated for subsets of
the sample because of its unusual composition and distribution. All headings with no topical subdivisions were removed
for one calculation because it was possible that the means
used to select most of the sample, i.e., elimination of all
headings with no subdivisions in the LC list, might possibly
have biased the sample. Furthermore, the unsubdivided
headings constituted nearly one-third of the entire sample
and might therefore have had a large influence on the results. As shown above, these conjectures were not verified;
the coefficients found for the entire sample and for this subset are reasonably close in value.

The two remaining subsets of the sample were used because it was outside these limits that the data became more
scattered (cf. Table 2); after the twenty-one-subdivision
level, there is a large gap; the ten-subdivision level is the
first instance where there is only one heading at a given
level. These subsets reduced the sample size of 339 cases

by seventeen and thirty-nine cases, respectively. It seemed
possible that other variables might have operated on these
scattered cases to reduce the coefficient somewhat. As can
be seen above, the coefficient was, instead, greater for the
entire sample--1.75 and 1.83 times as great, respectively.
The reason for this result would appear to be the great
spread in the lower portion of the distribution. The hypothesis did not posit a perfect correlation between number of
subdivisions and number of entries; in fact, another relationship was actually a part of the hypothesis (see next section).

This other relationship would also help to account for
the great spread in the lower portion of the distribution.
In this portion, a very few subdivisions of a sort that is
used whenever applicable, regardless of file length, would
produce a significant spread in the distribution. For instance, only five subdivisions of this nature, each applied to
a single title only, would suffice to place a heading in the
ten-subdivision category when without them it would have had
only five subdivisions, and the number of titles entered under
the heading would have remained much more typical of headings
with fewer subdivisions. Another variable which becomes significant when the difference in number of subdivisions is small is
the human one. Further subdivision of a file, under the
manual system in use at LC, is dependent on the need for
subdivision becoming apparent to a cataloger at a time when
he has both authority and time to initiate the change.

The first part of the hypothesis is supported: there is
a rather high, positive correlation between the number of
aspect subdivisions of a heading and the number of titles
entered under it; therefore, the subdivisions do tend to reduce file length.

Distinguishing Titles on a Particular Aspect of a Subject

No reliable evidence either to confirm or to deny this part of the hypothesis was found. There was, however, considerable evidence that a restatement might be valid. If the wording that "a factor in introduction of aspect subdivisions is the need to make manifest a significant number of books on a given aspect of the subject" is changed to " a factor in introduction of certain subdivisions is the need to make manifest the existence of books on a given aspect or in a given form of the subject, " there is evidence that with the new wording the proposition is valid. In the first place, form subdivisions are used whenever they are applicable, even if there is only one title under the heading. Usually the so-called aspect subdivisions which are actually accidents of terminology are applied regardless of the number of titles entered under the heading. Thus, there is every indication that once the decision was made to enter parts of airplanes under the heading Aeroplanes, subdivided by the name of the part, all books about parts of airplanes were so entered. When events are entered in the subdivision form under the name of the place where they occurred (Aachen - Siege, 1944; Messina - Earthquake, 1908), they are so entered even if a single title about the event is the only entry under the place name. There are certainly many other types of subdivisions applied in this way. It was, unfortunately, not possible to find firm evidence of application (or non-application) of true subdivisions (i.e., those indicating treatment not of a part or form of the subject, but treatment of the entire subject from a special point of view) in this manner.

Summary

The hypothesis tested was that two factors were present in use of aspect subdivisions of headings: (1) the need
to reduce file length under the heading; and (2) the need to
bring out the existence of a significant number of books on
a particular aspect, even if the total file was not particularly large. The first part of the hypothesis was supported on
the basis of a correlation of .675 between the number of
subdivisions (excluding form and geographical subdivisions)
and the number of entries in the LC official catalog under a
5 percent random sample of headings drawn from the LC
subject heading list.

No evidence could be found with regard to the second
part of the hypothesis in its original form, but when it was
modified to state that certain subdivisions were applied to
bring out the existence of titles in the area, regardless of
the total number of titles entered under the subject, support
for this proposition was found. There are several types of
subdivisions which are used when appropriate regardless of
the number of entries under the heading.

Notes

1.   Daily, "The Grammar of Subject Headings, " p. 119-120.

2.   Haykin, Subject Headings, p. 27.

3.   Ibid. , p. 27-36.

4.   While Haykin does not make the distinction in his dis-
     cussion, the last of these examples is not a time sub-
     division in the normal sense--i.e. , it includes not
     works limited in their scope to a certain period, but
     works published or composed in a certain period. Only
     subdivisions of the first type are arranged by date;

the example of the second type given in the text would
be filed among the alphabetical subdivisions of Aeronautics under E.

5.   Haykin, Subject Headings, p. 27.

6.   Ibid., p. 27-29.

7.   Ibid., p. 109-110.

8.   Haykin, Subject Headings, p. 29.

Chapter III

Adjective-Noun Phrases

When the subject of a book can be expressed by a single word, the problem of formation of the subject heading to express the subject is a relatively simple one. About the only choice required is between singular and plural--and this choice should be made on the basis of a policy decision, which in turn need generally be made only once.

The situation is much more complicated when it is not possible to express a concept by means of a single word. While there are more complex types of problems, probably the most important in terms of total number of concepts involved is that of ideas usually expressed in the form of adjectival phrases, such as acyloin reaction, Baroque art, airplane wings, and so on. While it would in theory be possible to use these phrases as subject headings in precisely the same form as they are given above, i.e., as a phrase composed of an adjective followed by a noun, such a policy is often not followed. Headings can be, and are, formed in a variety of ways from the terms given as examples above. These three concepts are structured as follows in the Library of Congress heading list:

> Acyloin reaction
> Art, Baroque
> Aeroplanes - Wings

These three examples represent the most common structural changes made in adjective-noun phrases in order to form

subject headings from them. They are entered (1) directly
in what might be called the natural language form with the
adjective preceding the noun; (2) inverted with the noun preceding the adjective; and (3) in the heading-subdivision form,
in which the adjective (in this case a noun used in an adjectival sense), is changed to the plural noun form, and the
noun follows it, the two words being separated by a dash.

No satisfactory rules for choosing among the available
alternatives for structuring adjectival phrases have ever been
developed, although the problem has been discussed in the
literature. Haykin does not mention the fact that many heading-subdivision combinations could be expressed as adjectival
phrases in natural language. He does state that inversion
is used "when it is desired to bring the noun in an adjectival heading into prominence, either in order that it may
appear in the catalog next to other headings beginning with
that noun, or because the adjective is used simply to differentiate between several headings on the same subject. "[1]
Tauber indicates that what evidence there is shows that library users state a preference for the direct form of heading when asked, but that they are as likely to approach a
heading indirectly as to approach it directly when actually
using the catalog. [2]

Frarey analyzed trends in subject heading structure
in the LC list for the decade 1941 to 1950 by comparing a
sample of the 1940 edition of the list with headings in the
supplements from 1941 to 1950. In 1940, 27.8 percent of
the total headings were direct adjectival phrases and 5.4
percent were inverted adjectival phrases. For the headings
added in the next decade the corresponding proportions were
26.6 percent and 5.6 percent. [3] These percentages are so

close as to indicate no change in policy with regard to inversion vs. direct entry of adjectival phrases during the
period under consideration.

Cutter preferred direct entry of adjectival phrases
except when another word was decidedly more important, but
he did admit that this principle was difficult to apply in
practice. [4] He cites Schwartz's noun rule, with examples,
as a rule which would be clear and easily followed, but to
which there are many objections. Schwartz's noun rule, as
described by Cutter, requires that adjectival phrases be, if
possible, "reduced to their equivalent nouns. "[5] Where this
is not possible the heading is inverted to bring the noun forward. Schwartz was librarian of the New York Apprentices'
Library and his noun rule was "carried out, with some exceptions [italics mine], in his catalog. "[6] Cutter does not
state what these exceptions were, although he does give a
list of terms such as Alimentary canal, inversion of which
would hardly be helpful.

The noun rule has been revived in recent years by
Prévost. [7] Her application of it goes far beyond a simple
inversion to bring the noun forward. Rather, the heading
is restructured to make "the direct subject noun"[8] the access point. International relations would thus become Nations - Interrelations. Prévost's justification of this method
is that application of the single rule would permit users always to know where to search in the catalog. It is highly
unlikely that her method would so operate in practice. The
subject of a book on international relations is not nations,
but rather the relationships among them.

If anything may be said to emerge from the discussions of structuring for adjectival phrase headings, it is that

no satisfactory rules exist. The appropriate position for a
new heading may be evident if it is simply an addition to a
group of exactly similar headings already in the heading list
or subject catalog, but if this is not the case, little guidance
for its placement is available.

Given the three major possibilities for structuring
adjectival phrase headings, the question arises as to whether
or not there are any constant factors influencing the choice
of heading form. Out of a multitude of possibilities, two
were selected for study.

The first is, taking as given that the heading is to
be expressed in the adjectival phrase form, what governs
the choice between the direct (Acyloin reaction) and the inverted (Art, Baroque) heading form? An hypothesis was
formulated that use of inverted adjective-noun combinations,
in preference to direct entry of these combinations, is dependent on which of the two words may be regarded as best
specifying the subject.

The second possibility is, taking as given that the
noun is to be brought forward to become the access point,
what governs the choice between the inverted adjectival
phrase form and the heading-subdivision form? An hypothesis was formulated that use of inverted adjective-noun
combinations, in preference to subdivision by means of the
dash, is used to achieve a classified subarrangement by
means of punctuation marks.

Inversion vs. Direct Entry

The hypothesis to be tested was that use of inverted
adjective-noun combinations, in preference to direct entry of
these combinations, is influenced by which of the two words

may be regarded as best specifying the subject. Subjective criteria might be set up to test this hypothesis, but past evidence shows that there are too many different varieties of headings and that interpretations of this sort are likely to be arbitrary and open to disagreement. It was necessary to devise a procedure or procedures which would permit a more objective approach to the problem.

The first procedure used was to take the list of inversions produced by the computer program described in Appendix II, and determine if the non-entry words brought forward in this listing were also used as entry words in the subject heading list. The see and see also references were used to provide a partial check on whether terms used as entry words in inversions were also used as non-entry words in headings entered directly. This analysis had two purposes: (1) to find those terms which either were always used as entry terms in adjective-noun phrases, or were never so used; and (2) for those terms whose use was mixed, i. e., they appeared both as entry and as non-entry words in adjective-noun combinations, to determine what pattern, if any, was present.

It early became clear that this approach would not provide useful results. Some terms are always the entry term (Insurance; Baths); fewer never are (Instruments). Some are always the entry term except when what might be regarded as a term of higher precedence is part of the heading. For instance, almost all adjective-noun headings using Art as either of these parts of speech use that word as the entry term, but there are a few exceptions, such as Insurance, Art.

While it was possible to set up a listing of those

words which were preferred as entry or non-entry words,
together with an indication of precedence when two such
words co-occurred, there was no pattern evident; that is, a
prediction of the order of precedence in other adjective-noun
headings was not made possible.

Results were similar for those terms whose use was
mixed; that is, they were sometimes used as entry terms
and sometimes not. No pattern was clear. For these reasons, this approach was abandoned with the conclusion that
no pattern of preference could be shown with regard to the
words themselves in these combinations.

The inspection involved in this analysis led to another
approach. It would seem possible that if an adjective-noun
combination were selected as describing a subject, the less
common of the two words might be regarded as best specifying the subject, in accordance with Shannon and Weaver's
demonstration that the amount of information provided by a
message is related inversely to the probability of its occurrence.[9] Since we are dealing with a general subject heading
list, frequency of occurrence in normal running text would
have to be the criterion of "commonness." This is not to
say that frequency of occurrence of the terms in headings is
explicitly considered by the cataloger in determining whether
to enter the heading in a direct or an inverted form.
Rather, the "commonness" of a word might enter into the
decision. If this were true, then a comparison of the frequencies of entry and non-entry words in adjective-noun
combinations ought to show a significant difference.

Fortunately, a word-frequency listing based on a
large sample of running text in present-day American English was available. This is the so-called "million-word

corpus, " the Standard Corpus of Present-Day Edited American English, assembled at Brown University and available in
machine-readable form. A book describing the characteristics of the Corpus includes an alphabetical list of every word
appearing in the Corpus, together with its frequency of
occurrence. [10]

Since subject headings are based on natural language
but are actually only a formalized subset of natural language,
a simple listing of the frequencies of the actual forms of
words used in subject headings would not be adequate. Both
the singular and the plural of noun forms of words were
counted; hyphenated words were listed as one and as two
words, and frequencies given for both; if a common alternative spelling existed the frequencies for both spellings
were used.

Certain limitations were also placed on the headings
used in the analysis. Only used main headings of the form
[adjective or word used in an adjectival sensel] space [noun],
or [noun] comma space [adjective or word used in an adjectival sense] were considered. Thus, Meteorological instruments; English literature; and Art, Hindu were all used,
but such headings as Teachers, Professional ethics for;
Insurance, War risk; and Decoration and ornament, Mohammedan were omitted. Hyphenated compound words were regarded as two words and the preceding rule was applied.
The limitation was made because two difficulties arise if
complex forms are included: the different forms are not
always directly comparable with each other; and the decision
as to which of the possibilities is to be regarded as the adjective and as the noun, and which ignored, is a difficult
one and would have to be more or less arbitrary in many

cases.   The procedure chosen reduced the size of the
sample somewhat, but insured greater comparability.

The frequency of occurrence for both the entry and
the non-entry words was listed for each heading of the types
under consideration.   Since adjectives denoting national,
ethnic, cultural, or linguistic distinctions clearly form a
special case--and a large proportion of the headings--these
were tabulated separately.   (The term "national adjective"
is used to include all of these, although some of the adjectives do not denote nationality.)   Thus there were four categories of headings:

> Direct non-national adjective
> Inverted non-national adjective
> Direct national adjective
> Inverted national adjective

Several preliminary analyses of the results were performed in order to find the most useful method.   Table 3
summarizes the data on which these analyses were performed.   The first section (Ungrouped data) includes the
total number of headings in the sample by category; the total
and mean frequencies for entry and for non-entry words in
each category; and the percentage of headings in each category in which the frequency of the entry word was greater
than that of the non-entry word.   A difference in frequency
between entry and non-entry words is clear in only one category (direct national adjective) in this section of the table.

It was found in compiling the frequency data that certain high-frequency terms such as Art and Music, which appear as the entry word in many headings in each category
and, therefore, were counted many times, were affecting the
results significantly.   Since using the "commonness" of a
word as a criterion for its degree of specification of a sub-

TABLE 3. Word frequencies in adjective-noun combinations[a]

	Total headings	Frequencies total E	Frequencies total NE	mean E	mean NE	E frequency greater than NE (%)
I. Ungrouped data						
Direct non-national	938	90,479	107,449	96	115	41%
Inverted non-national	192	15,914	14,179	83	74	54%
Direct national	259	3,844	29,921	15	116	8%
Inverted national	96	7,865	7,428	82	77	53%
II. Grouped data						95% confidence limits
Direct non-national	414	16,329	48,528	39	117	17% + 3.6%
Inverted non-national	62	3,185	3,844	51	62	37% + 9.8%
Direct national	154	336	19,651	2	128	1% + 1.5%
Inverted national	18	681	1,910	38	106	22% + 19.0%

[a]Symbols: E = entry word
NE = non-entry word

ject involves an assumption that one purpose is to reduce
the total number of entries beginning with the same word,
the data were analyzed differently as shown in Section II
(Grouped data) of Table 3. In this section, each different
entry word is counted only once, and the mean of all the
non-entry words appearing with that word is used for comparison. The effect of the words which are used in many
headings is clear when one compares the two sections of the
table. Furthermore, in most cases it would appear from
inspection that there is a significant difference between the
mean frequencies of the entry and the non-entry words in
each category. The proportion of entry words more common than the corresponding non-entry words is also far
lower. Use of the grouped data permits, for practical purposes, elimination of a subcategory of headings (those which
are part of long files beginning with the same word), so that
the special characteristics of these headings do not mask the
relationships which are actually of concern. For this reason tests of significance were carried out on the mean frequencies of the grouped data only.

Table 3 shows (for the grouped data only) the limits,
at the 95 percent confidence level, of the percentage of headings in which the frequency of the entry word was greater
than that of the non-entry word. Since this measure[11] is
greatly influenced by the size of the sample, the limits are
much broader for the two categories of inverted headings
than for the direct headings. If, in as many as 47 percent
of the inverted non-national adjectival headings the entry-
word frequency may be greater than that of the non-entry
word, it cannot be said with any confidence that these headings were inverted to bring forward the less common word.

However, this comparison is clearly valid for the direct non-national headings, since the entry word is more common than the non-entry word in only 21 percent of these headings at most. The form of headings containing a national adjective is determined mainly by characteristics other than frequency, as will be shown later. It is, however, interesting that the entry word is not likely to be the more common word of the pair in either direct or inverted headings containing a national adjective.

Differences between mean frequencies

The mean frequencies were compared to determine if, at the 95 percent confidence level, the pairs of means described below were actually different. In each case, the non-national and the national adjectival headings were compared only with each other. Each mean was compared with two other means: the entry word was compared with the non-entry word in each category, and a cross-comparison was made between equivalent terms in direct and inverted headings, i.e., the entry word in direct headings was compared with the non-entry word in inverted headings, and vice-versa. The first comparisons were intended to show if the less common adjectives were entered directly while the more common ones were inverted, and the reverse for the nouns; while the second set of comparisons was intended to show if the less common adjectives and nouns each tended to be the entry words, while the more common ones became non-entry words. Since inspection of the means for non-national adjectival headings made it appear highly possible that the only mean which was reliably different from the others was that for non-entry words in direct headings, the calculations were extended to include all possible pairs of means in the non-national headings category.

Fig. 1 shows the range of possible differences, at
the 95 percent level of confidence, between each pair of
means involved.   Table 4 presents the same data in a different form, showing the two means in each comparison, the
observed difference between the two means, the limits of the
difference between the means at the 95 percent confidence
level, and the range within which the true difference falls
according to these limits.

Ranges of values in Fig. 1 which lie entirely above
the zero axis of the graph indicate that at the 95 percent
confidence level the greater of the observed means is actually the greater true mean.   Those ranges which extend below
the zero axis indicate that the greater of the observed means
may or may not actually be the smaller of the two means,
to the extent shown.   Thus, when the observed mean for
entry words in direct non-national headings (39.4) is compared with that for non-entry words in inverted non-national
headings (62), Fig. 1 shows a range of -17 to +63 for the
difference between the means, indicating that at this confidence level the greater of the observed means may actually
be anywhere from 17 less to 63 greater in value than the
lesser of the observed means.

These ranges are all fairly great, due probably to
two characteristics of the data: (1) the number of items in
some of the categories of the sample (especially inverted
headings) is quite small; and (2) the variability in frequency
in all categories is quite high, as would be expected to be
the case if the hypothesis were correct--that is, that word
frequency is one influence in selection of the entry term in
adjective-noun subject headings.   The variability would, of

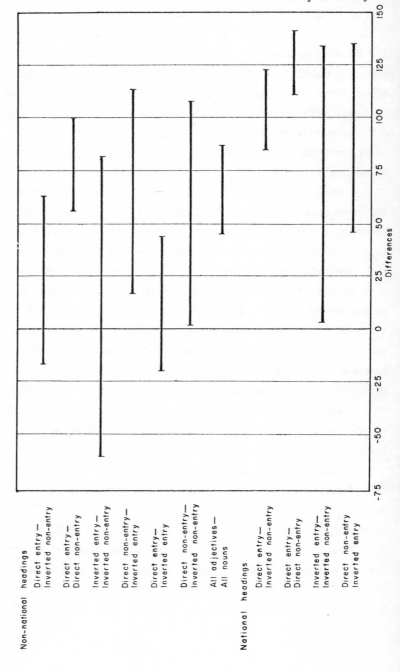

FIGURE I.—Difference between mean frequencies, 95% confidence level

TABLE 4: Comparison of mean frequencies: 95 % confidence level

Categories compared	No. of Hdgs.	Observed mean frequencies	Difference between means		
			Observed difference	95 % confidence limits	Range of true difference
I. Non-national headings					
Direct entry	414	39.4	77.6	$\pm$22.0	55.6 - 99.6
Direct non-entry	414	117			
Direct non-entry	414	117	65.6	$\pm$48.2	17.4 - 113.8
Inverted entry	62	51.4			
Direct non-entry	414	117	55.0	$\pm$53.3	1.7 - 108.3
Inv. non-entry	62	62.0			
Direct entry	414	39.4	12.0	$\pm$31.9	-19.9 - +43.9
Inverted entry	62	51.4			
Direct entry	414	39.4	22.6	$\pm$40.0	-17.4 - +62.6
Inv. non-entry	62	62.0			
Inverted entry	62	51.4	10.6	$\pm$70.9	-60.3 - +81.5
Inv. non-entry	62	62.0			
All adjectives	476	42.3	66.2	$\pm$20.9	45.3 - 87.1
All nouns	476	108.5			

TABLE 4: Continued

Categories compared	No. of Hdgs.	Observed mean frequencies	Difference between means		
			Observed difference	95% confidence limits	Range of true difference
II. National headings					
Direct entry	154	2.2	125.8	±15.1	110.7 - 140.9
Direct non-entry	154	128			
Direct entry	154	2.2	103.8	±18.7	85.1 - 122.5
Inv. non-entry	18	106			
Direct non-entry	154	128	90.2	±44.4	45.8 - 134.6
Inverted entry	18	37.8			
Inverted entry	18	37.8	68.2	±65.5	2.7 - 133.7
Inv. non-entry	18	106			

course, also be very high if the hypothesis were incorrect; that is, if word frequency were not an influence at all on selection of entry term in these phrases. However, as discussed in the next two sections, the actual characteristics of the means make it appear likely that word frequency is a factor, although either it is not one of precisely the sort suggested by the hypothesis, or other factors tend to obscure the hypothesized relationship.

Comparison of means in non-national adjectival headings

The mean frequency of non-entry words in direct headings is greater than all other mean frequencies in the non-national category at the 95 percent confidence level. However, the minimum difference of 1.7 between non-entry words in direct and in inverted headings can hardly be regarded as significant. The only interpretation which may safely be made from these data is that when the noun in an adjective-noun heading is much more common that the adjective, the heading is likely to be entered directly, i.e., adjective first. The evidence from which this interpretation is drawn is that the nouns (non-entry words) in direct headings are much more common than either the adjectives (entry words) in these headings, or the nouns (entry words) in inverted headings. It would appear that when the difference between the frequency of the adjective and that of the noun is not great, the tendency is to invert the heading. The evidence on this last point is, however, entirely negative, as it is based on the lack of a significant difference between the means.

Since adjectives might be of less frequent occurrence than nouns in natural language, the mean frequency for all

adjectives (i. e. , direct entry plus inverted non-entry words)
was compared with that of all nouns (i. e. , direct non-entry
plus inverted entry words) in the non-national heading category; the results are also shown in Table 4 and Fig. 1. At
the 95 percent confidence level, the mean frequency of the
nouns is at least double that of the adjectives.

If word frequency in natural language were the influence in selection of the entry term, of if the same relationship (between frequency of adjectives and of nouns) held in
subject headings (a subset of natural language), the greater
frequency of nouns would have no effect on the choice of
entry term in adjective-noun headings. However, it could
be postulated that the frequency of an adjective relative to
other adjectives, or of a noun relative to other nouns, might
be the influence which helped to determine the selection of
the entry term in a given case. Any attempts to test this
possibility with the data available, however, would lead to
nebulous conclusions at best. The evidence available
clearly suggests that word frequency in natural language
is related to selection of the entry term in non-national
adjective-noun combinations, and the hypothesis that
choice of entry term for these combinations is influenced
by whichever of the two words may be best regarded as
specifying the subject is partially and tentatively supported.

Comparison of means in national adjectival headings

The mean frequencies of terms used in national adjectival headings present an entirely different picture from
those of the non-national headings. Reference to Table 4
and Fig. 1 makes this clear. At the 95 percent confidence
level the greater of the observed means is also the greater

of the true means in all four comparisons. In only one
instance, comparison of inverted entry with inverted non-
entry words, does the range of the true difference extend so
close to zero as to give rise to any doubt as to the importance of the difference, and in this case the small number of
cases in the sample (18) contributes greatly to the broad
range.

The small number of different nouns actually used as
entry terms in inverted national adjectival headings is perhaps one of the most striking findings of this analysis. The
eighteen such terms which appeared in this 10 percent sample
of the subject heading list are:

Actresses
Art
Baths
Costume
Firearms
Hygiene
Inscriptions
Inventors
Journalists
Litterateurs
Magic
Maxims
Medalists
Medals
Music
Propaganda
Quatrains
Revolutionists

By extrapolation, there must be less than 200 such terms in
the entire subject heading list. Some of them fall into clear
categories. When a national specification is added to a term
describing some class of human beings, the heading is always inverted (e.g., Actresses, English; Revolutionists,
German). This category accounts for one-third (6) of the
headings in this group. When a national specification is

applied to certain very minor literary forms, it is also inverted. This accounts for <u>Maxims</u> and <u>Quatrains</u>. The remaining terms are difficult to account for, except that they
tend to be among those which are always, or nearly always,
the entry term, not only in adjective-noun combinations but
in other heading forms also.

The nouns used in direct national adjectival headings
show a different pattern from those used in inverted headings. There are more different terms, but the two words
<u>language</u> and <u>literature</u> are the nouns used in the vast ma-
jority of all the direct headings; and other literary forms
such as <u>poetry</u> and <u>drama,</u> and <u>culture</u> account for the bulk
of the remainder.

One characteristic of headings in which an adjective
denoting an ethnic, national, linguistic, or cultural distinction is used is very important. In all cases but one the
noun is the determinant of direct or inverted entry. That
is, if a given noun is the entry word, and the adjective is
inverted, all headings composed of this noun and a national
adjective are inverted. The converse is true: if a given
noun is not the entry word in one such heading, it never is.
The sole exception found in this study was the adjective
<u>Negro.</u> It is entered directly in conjunction with several
nouns which in all other instances are entered in the inverted form. No explanation of this one special case was
attempted.

Given the fact that the noun is the determining factor
in the choice between direct and inverted entry of national
adjectival headings, some further conclusions may tentatively
be drawn. It seems quite likely that those nouns with which
it is likely that only "important" national adjectives (such as

English or French, but not Kechua or Kate) would be used
would be entered in the inverted form, i.e., with the noun
first. These important national adjectives are also those of
higher frequency in natural language. Conversely, those
nouns which are used with a great many national adjectives,
most of them of low frequency, are likely to be entered di-
rectly--the adjective first.

However, while the evidence for these conclusions is
clear from the subject heading list, caution in interpretation
is necessary. Headings containing national adjectives are
represented in the list as examples in many cases. This is
particularly true in the case of inverted headings, where the
form

Actresses, American, [English, French, etc.]

is very common. It is conceivable that in the actual catalog
of the Library of Congress the distinctions made above do
not hold true. However, this does seem unlikely.

Inversion vs. Subdivision

The hypothesis to be tested was that inversions and
subdivisions are used to create a classed subarrangement of
headings which are otherwise the same up to the comma or
the dash, in keeping with Haykin's statement that an inversion is a kind of subdivision. [12] For this purpose, all the
headings in the sample which contained both inversions and
subdivisions were listed and the inversions and subdivisions
analyzed. Headings for which the only subdivisions were
geographic were excluded from the analysis on the grounds
that the classed sub-arrangement feature is self evident in
this case. (Geographic subdivisions are always filed after
all other subdivisions.) With this exclusion, there were a

total of ninety-three headings in the sample which were subdivided and were also followed by inverted headings which
were identical up to the comma, including both see references and used headings. These headings are:

Actresses
Aeroplanes
Agricultural laborers
Agricultural laws and
   legislation
Algae
Algebra
Archives
Art
Art industries and
   trade
Art metal-work
Art objects
Association, insti-
   tutions, etc.
Anthropology
Bowling
Cataloging
Cities and towns
Clergy
Costume
Crustacea
Decision-making
Decoration and
   ornament
Drugs
Electricity
Entomology
Fasts and feasts
Fathers of the
   Church
Flies
Gardens
Gas
Generative organs
Grain elevators
Hematology
Holidays
Hygiene
Income tax

Insane
Insanity
Insurance
Inventions
Inventories
Inventors
Invertebrates
Journalism
Journalists
Judaism
Letter-writing
Light
Liturgies
Magic
Marriage
Medals
Meteorology
Milking-machines
Mushrooms
Music
Nobility
Noise
Oboe with orchestra
Oboe with string orchestra
Orders of knighthood
   and chivalry
Ordnance
Paper
Plankton
Planning
Playgrounds
Pleading
Questions and answers
Revivals
Rubber
Schism
Science
Science fiction
Snails
Snakes

Social service	Theater
State, The	Therapeutics
Supervisors	Touch
Sweet potatoes	Treaties
Swine	Trumpet with orchestra
Syphilis	Tuberculosis
Teachers	Typewriting
Technical assistance	Valves
Textile fibers	Vocal Music
Textile industry and fabrics	

While production of classed sub-arrangements <u>may</u> be a factor in the choice between subdivision and inversion of headings, the structure of language is certainly a factor. Usually subdivisions are nouns or nominative phrases, while inversions are usually adjectives or adjectival phrases. However, often the same concept could be expressed either way, and a choice must be made. Proof of this may be found in the sizable number of cases where reference is made from the subdivided to the inverted heading form, or vice-versa; for example:

> Agricultural laws and legislation - Colonies
> See Agricultural laws and legislation, Colonial

On the other hand, sometimes the same word is used in both its adjectival form as inversion and its noun form as subdivision, but with a different scope. This is true primarily of terms denoting nationality, used with such headings as <u>Art</u>. In this case <u>Art - France</u> includes art which is physically located in France, while <u>Art, French</u> includes the art of France (although there is no way to determine from the subject heading list whether the scope of the heading actually includes only art produced within the borders of France by French artists, art produced anywhere in the world by French artists, art produced in France by artists of all nationalities, or the last two of the preceding possi-

bilities). However, there is nothing inherent in the structure of language or of subject headings to require this distinction. The Sears subject heading list, for example, uses
the inverted form for both kinds of material.

Inspection of the terms used in adjectival inversions
and in subdivisions indicates that in at least some cases the
subdivisions are used to indicate publication and other forms
(e.g., Botany - Dictionaries), and also the aspect or point
of view from which the subject is treated (e.g., Grain elevators - Fires and fire prevention), while the inverted form
describes a subclass of the subject. (In the case of Grain
elevators, for example, it is possible to distinguish Grain
elevators, Cooperative from all other Grain elevators, while
Fires and fire prevention as a subdivision applies to all
Grain elevators.)

Of the 93 headings analyzed, a total of 68, or just
under 75 percent, were clearly subdivided only by aspect
and/or form, while all the inversions referred to specific
kinds. Seven additional headings were subdivided only by
aspect or form, and were modified only by the single term
Fossil, e.g., Algae, Fossil. A fine distinction must be
drawn in order to say that the scope of this heading is a
particular kind of algae--or even to state unequivocally that
fossil algae are actually algae at all. However, regardless
of these semantic and technical distinctions, the use of the
inverted form does provide a classified sub-arrangement, so
that the total number of headings in which all the inversions
and subdivisions indicate a classed sub-arrangement is increased to 75, about 80 percent of the headings in the
sample.

Another five headings meet the criteria specified,

with the exception of cross references. In one of these
cases the cross reference is from a subdivision which represents a kind to the inverted form of the same heading:

> Agricultural laws and legislation - Colonies
>   See Agricultural laws and legislation, Colonial

Another has cross references from a kind as both subdivision and inversion to another heading:

> Holidays - Jews
>   See Fasts and feasts - Judaism
> Holidays, Jewish
>   See Fasts and feasts - Judaism

Under another heading the structure of references under subdivisions and inversions is as follows:

> Milling-machines - Numerical control
> x Milling machines - Punched tape control
>   Milling-machines, Tape-controlled
>   Numerically controlled milling-machines
>   Robot milling-machines
>   Tape-controlled milling-machines
>   ·
>   Milling-machines - Punched tape control
>   See Milling-machines - Numerical control
>   Milling-machines - Safety measures
>   Milling-machines, Tape-controlled
>   See Milling-machines - Numerical control

This set of headings is a clear case where both noun (subdivision) and adjectival (inverted) headings were available.
The subdivision actually used (Numerical control) implies an
aspect, but the references to this subdivision clearly imply
that the scope is an actual class of milling-machines. Perhaps the best lesson to be drawn from this example is that
the distinction between as aspect and a class is not always
cut-and-dried.

The two remaining headings which meet the criteria
for the subdivision-aspect and inversion-kind distinction with
the exception of cross references are:

86 Subject Analysis

Art - Negroes
    See Negro art
Insanity - Negroes
    See Negroes - Insanity

The first of these references represents a kind of class of art; the second, however, certainly does not represent a kind of insanity, but rather insanity among a special group of people.

If these five headings, which are prevented only by a cross reference or two from full compliance with the criteria, are accepted, then a total of 80 out of 93 headings, or over 85 percent of the headings in the sample, use the form of classed sub-arrangement in which subdivisions are used for forms and aspects from which the subject is treated and inversions are used for special kinds of subclasses of the subject.

The remaining thirteen headings, some of which show evidence of the subdivision-inversion distinction being used to achieve the same classed sub-arrangement, but with some exceptions, or to achieve a different classed sub-arrangement, are

Aeroplanes	Hygiene
Clergy	Income tax
Decoration and	Journalism
ornament	Marriage
Electricity	Music
Fasts and feasts	Schism
Hematology	Theater

Of these headings, nine fulfill the criteria used, except that some kinds or classes are used as subdivisions. These are (giving only the subdivisions which represent kinds or classes):

Clergy
    - Major orders
    See Bishops
        Clergy
    - Minor orders

Decoration and ornament
 - Empire style
 - Louis XIV style
 - Louis XV style
 - Louis XVI style
Fasts and feasts
 - Catholic Church, [Church of England, Presbyterian
     Church, etc.]
 - Hinduism
 - Jews
     See Fasts and feasts - Judaism
 - Judaism
 - Mohammedanism
Income tax - Foreign income
Journalism
 - Agriculture
     See Journalism, Agricultural
 - Automobile industry and trade
 - Automobiles
 - Commerce
     See Journalism, Commercial
 - Labor
     See Journalism, Labor
 - Medicine
     See Journalism, Medical
 - Negroes
     See Negro press
 - Religion
     See Journalism, Religious
 - Sports
     See Sports journalism
Marriage
 - Anglican Communion
     See Marriage - Church of England
         Marriage - Protestant Episcopal Church
             in the U. S. A.
 - Catholic Church
 - Church of England
 - Jews
 - Lutheran Church, [New Jerusalem Church, etc.]
 - Mohammedanism
 - Orthodox Eastern Church
 - Protestant Episcopal Church in the U. S. A.

Music
- Negroes
- Sunday-schools
  See Sunday-schools - Hymns
Schism
- Eastern and Western Church
- Greek and Latin Church
  See Schism - Eastern and Western Church
  Schism, Acacian, 484-519
- Latin and Greek Church
  See Schism - Eastern and Western Church
  Schism, Acacian, 484-519
Theater - Little theater movement

The subdivisions of <u>Clergy</u>, <u>Decoration and ornament</u>, <u>Income tax</u>, <u>Marriage</u>, <u>Schism</u> and <u>Theater</u> listed above are all terms which it would not be feasible to put in the adjectival form for inversion. Furthermore, the subdivisions of <u>Decoration and ornament</u> and <u>Schism</u> are the only subdivisions of these headings shown in the subject heading list; while the subdivisions of <u>Marriage</u> are listed in a sub-arrangement separate from all other subdivisions. Therefore the classified sub-arrangement principle is carried out in part for these three headings. The subdivisions and inversions (the latter are not listed here, but are evident from the cross references) of <u>Journalism</u> show a preference for the inverted form for <u>kinds</u> of journalism (as predicted by the criteria). The subdivision form is used for terms which could not conveniently be expressed in the inverted form; the references from the subdivided to the inverted form show evidence of an attempt to provide access to all kinds of journalism from a single file. There is, however, no reference in this file to:

Journalism, Military
Journalism, Pictorial
Journalism, Prison
Journalism, Scientific

Journalism, Socialist
Journalism, Technical

The subdivisions shown above for <u>Fasts and feasts</u> are the
only ones given in the subject heading list.   These clearly
fall in the category of "special subdivisions" which are likely
to be filed separately, thus carrying out the classified sub-
arrangement.   There is no clear reason for use of the subdivided form with the remaining heading, <u>Music</u>.

There are four more headings which did not meet the
classified sub-arrangement criteria given above.   These are:

Aeroplanes
Electricity
Hematology
Hygiene

The subdivisions of <u>Aeroplanes</u> are mainly for parts of airplanes, e. g., <u>Aeroplanes - Wings</u>, but include aspect and
form subdivisions.   There is one subdivision, however, the
cross reference to which is reminiscent of those to <u>Milling-
machines - Numerical control</u>, in that the form of the subdivision implies an aspect or a part, but the cross reference
implies that it is a special class.   This is:

Aeroplanes - Jet propulsion
x Aeroplanes, Jet propelled

The subdivisions for other forms of propulsion do not have
equivalent cross references.   In addition, the inverted airplane headings, such as <u>Aeroplanes, Company</u> and <u>Aero-
planes, Military</u> are not all really <u>kinds</u> of aircraft, but they
could be regarded as <u>classes</u>; class membership might be
accidental and subject to change, but each class can be distinguished from other classes.

All the inversions under <u>Electricity</u> are cross references; all may be regarded as kinds except

Electricity, Medical
    See Electrotherapeutics

which represents an application.

Under <u>Hematology</u> the two inversions are cross re-ferences:

Hematology, Forensic
    See Forensic hematology
Hematology, Veterinary
    See Veterinary hematology

It would require a fine distinction to say whether these re-present aspects or special branches of the subject. Regard-less, they are a separate group in meaning.

The situation with regard to <u>Hygiene</u> is identical to that for <u>Hematology</u> except that there are more inversions, and both used headings and see references are involved.

With certain exceptions it may be stated that the choice between inversion and subdivision of headings is made to produce a classified sub-arrangement.

<u>Summary</u>

<u>Inversion vs. direct entry</u>

Based on word frequency in natural language as a criterion of degree of specification, the hypothesis that the choice between inversion and direct entry of adjectival phrases is influenced by which word best specifies the sub-ject is supported to a very limited extent when non-national adjectives are involved. It is certain that when the fre-quency of the noun is much greater than that of the adjec-tive, the phrase will usually be entered directly, i.e., ad-jective first. It is also clear that less frequently occurring nouns are much more likely to become the entry word in adjectival phrases than those occurring more frequently.

Based on the lack of a significant difference between the
nouns and the adjectives in inverted phrases, and between
the adjectives in inverted and in direct phrases, it would
appear that there might be a tendency to bring the noun forward by inverting adjectival phrases unless the noun is of
much greater frequency than the adjective.

In adjective-noun phrases where the adjective denotes
nationality, language, culture, or ethnic grouping, the difference between mean frequency of entry and non-entry words
is significant in all cases. Word frequency is clearly a
major influence in structuring these phrases.

In all adjectival phrases the word frequency is associated with the selection of the entry term; it is certainly
not the only influence, and it is perfectly possible that some
other factor which also happens to be associated with word
frequency is the determining one. Nevertheless, in structuring new subject headings the relative frequencies of the
words involved ought to be a valuable indicator of the degree
of specification afforded by each alternative.

Inversion vs. subdivision

The hypothesis that inversions and subdivisions of
headings are used to produce a classified sub-arrangement
was in large part supported. Eighty percent of the headings
in the sample used subdivisions for aspect or form, and inversions for kinds or subclasses of the subject, while in the
remaining 20 percent a classed sub-arrangement with small
exceptions, or a sub-arrangement using different or additional classes, was present.

Notes

1. Haykin, Subject Headings, p. 22.

2. Maurice F. Tauber, et al., Technical Services in Libraries, p. 169.

3. Frarey, "Subject Heading Revision," p. 26.

4. Cutter, Rules, 4th ed., p. 72.

5. Ibid.

6. Ibid.

7. Prévost, "Approach to Theory and Method," p. 140-151.

8. Ibid., p. 143.

9. Warren Weaver, "Recent Contributions to the Mathematical Theory of Communication," in The Mathematical Theory of Communication, by Claude E. Shannon and Warren Weaver, p. 15.

10. Henry Kučera and W. Nelson Francis, Computational Analysis of Present-Day American English, p. 139-271.

11. John I. Griffin, Statistics: Methods and Applications, p. 182-183.

12. Haykin, Subject Headings, p. 84.

Chapter IV

Relative Scope of Headings for Use in
Different Types of Collections

To judge from some of the literature, the needs of
the clientele of various types of libraries vary to such an
extent that no broad principles of subject analysis would be
useful.[1] In particular, it is often said that among libraries
whose subject scope is more or less general the smaller
ones, such as school and small public libraries, need broader subject headings than larger public and research libraries.
Furthermore, it is probably true that a library specializing
in a particular subject will require headings different from
those required by a library the subject scope of whose collection is general.

The assumption that users' needs vary according to
the level of the collection involved is part of the rationale
behind the existence of more than one general subject heading list. In addition, the question periodically arises of the
need for a separate list of subject headings for children's
collections along the lines of the Rue-LaPlante list of some
years ago.[2]

However, the assumptions that smaller libraries need
broader subject headings, and that the subject heading which
should be applied to a book is the one which best and most
precisely describes what the book is about, come into direct
conflict. A given book is about the same subject whether it
is cataloged for a small or a large library, or for a child-

ren's or an adult's collection.

This is most certainly not to imply that a comparison of the subject catalogs of two collections varying in age level and/or size would not show that, in general, the subject headings appearing in one were more specialized than those in the other. It may be assumed that the level of specialization of the materials in a larger or more advanced collection would be such as to require more specialized subject headings.

It is important to determine if the level of size of the collection for which cataloging is intended to provide access has actually influenced the subject headings assigned to materials. For this purpose it would be necessary to compare the subject headings assigned to the same book titles in cataloging designed for different types of collections.

Jackson has reported on a study of the difference in broadness or narrowness between subject headings applied to the same books by the Wilson Company and the Library of Congress.[3] However, the purpose of his study was to determine the relative scope of the headings available in the Sears and LC lists. His sample was made up of two parts: (1) a stratified random sample of over 700 adult nonfiction titles from the Standard Catalog for Public Libraries, fourth edition; and (2) all the adult nonfiction titles, except individual biography, from the 1958-1960 supplement to the High School Catalog (about 400 titles); a total of about 1,150 titles. The subject headings assigned by Wilson in these catalogs were compared with the headings given for the same books in the Library of Congress National Union Catalog of Books: Authors. Whenever there was a difference, the Sears list was checked to see what headings were available.

Jackson's analysis is based on the headings available for use, not those assigned, and he does not distinguish differences in scope of the headings themselves from limitation to a single aspect by means of subdivision. All the comparisons were in terms of matched pairs of headings, one pair per title. Many books of course have more than one subject heading, and it is almost certain that there were some headings applied by one of the services which had no counterpart among the headings applied to the same books by the other. Since these facts are not mentioned in the report it is not possible to judge how many of these there were, or what their significance might have been. Furthermore, limitation of the study to adult nonfiction, while it probably permits concentration on the relative scope of the headings available for use, eliminates from consideration a major part of the cataloging burden of any smaller library, fiction and non-adult titles.

Jackson's results do show, however, that the differences between LC and Sears headings are not as great as has sometimes been supposed. He presents a full breakdown of the kinds of differences he encountered, but shows the relative importance of the broad categories only.

In another study an analysis was made of 100 subject headings applied to books in the catalog of a library which uses LC cards but applies subject headings from the Rue-LaPlante list to the titles in its juvenile collection. Of these 100 headings, 31 were headings from the Library of Congress card accepted without change, while another 41 were headings from the Library of Congress card, shortened by deletion of a qualifier, usually Juvenile literature. The 28 Rue headings added were in many cases acceptable LC headings with the qualifier Stories added. [4]

The objective of the study reported here was to determine whether choice of the subject heading proper (exclusive of aspect subdivisions) for application to the same books is or is not dependent on the nature, size, or objectives of the general library collections for which subject cataloging is designed.

The cataloging of a particular library is likely to be influenced by local factors extraneous to the issue at hand; it is therefore preferable to test the hypothesis on the cataloging produced by major services, which is intended to be useful to a variety of libraries. The cards produced by the Library of Congress and the H. W. Wilson Company fit this need. The former is intended for advanced and research collections and uses the LC list of subject headings; the latter for school and smaller public libraries and uses the Sears list. Other services, such as Alanar and LJ cards, produce cataloging for smaller libraries, but the Wilson service has been in existence the longest and therefore probably has cataloged the largest universe of titles. Where Alanar DS cards[5] were available for titles in the sample, their subject headings were compared for illustrative purposes.

The main requirement for carrying out the study was a universe of book titles for which both Wilson and Library of Congress subject cataloging were available. It was preferable that the titles in the universe not vary too much in publication date (to avoid bias produced by policy changes, if any), and that the universe be composed of relatively recent titles (since present practice is the issue). By definition, the sample would not be representative as far as LC

cataloging is concerned: LC catalogs many titles of a nature
that is outside the Wilson Company's scope.   The sample
should be representative of Wilson cataloging within any
limits set.

A universe which is essentially randomly ordered
with regard to any characteristic that might affect the assignment of subject headings is to be preferred.   This would
avoid the necessity of introducing stratification or other
means of preventing bias.   A universe fulfilling the needs
was made available by Alanar, Inc., a book supplier which
provides cataloging for its books.   Catalog cards for their
most active titles are kept in a file arranged first by pub-
lisher and then (roughly) by title.   All types of catalog cards
which Alanar has available for a given title are kept in this
file.   This includes Library of Congress, Wilson and two
types of Alanar cards.   Since the most active titles tend to
be the newer ones, and since Alanar has not been supplying
cards for very many years, the titles in their file are
mostly recent.   1960 was selected somewhat arbitrarily as
a cutoff date before which no title would be included in the
sample.   It was about this year that Alanar began supplying
cataloging on a large scale, and a preliminary check showed
that this cutoff date would include nearly all of the titles in
the file.   The eight-year span would not be long enough for
a high likelihood of major cataloging policy changes.   The
date used was that in the Library of Congress card number.
This date, for recent popular materials, usually corresponds
quite closely with the copyright date.   Use of it removes
problems of books with no date, or with more than one.
Furthermore, it indicates when the book was cataloged, at
least by the Library of Congress, and thus assures that the

problem of policy changes has not crept in. Use of a date
appearing only on the LC card prevented any titles for which
no LC cards were available from being sampled. However,
this eliminated only a very few titles, and, with no LC subject headings, they would have been useless anyway.

The catalog cards in this file are stored in boxes,
and the boxes were sampled by assigning numbers from one
to 4,162 to them, and then taking computer-generated random numbers to determine which boxes were to appear in
the sample.

In order to determine the size of the universe, a 2
percent random sample (80 boxes) was taken. Those titles
in these boxes which had LC card dates from 1960 to 1968
were divided into two categories, those without and those
with Wilson cards, and the number of titles in each category
was determined. The mean number of titles per box for
which there were no Wilson cards was 6.64; the mean for
those with Wilson cards was 2.22. The total number in
each category (rounded to the nearest 100) is 27,600 and
9,300, respectively, or a total of 36,900 titles dated 1960
or later.

In order to compare LC and Wilson subject headings
a 10 percent random sample of the 4,162 boxes was drawn.
From each of the boxes used, the first title with an LC card
date of 1960 or later, and for which there were also Wilson
cards, was drawn for the sample. If a given box contained
no title fulfilling these qualifications, no cards were drawn
from it. From the 401 boxes in the sample, 294 titles were
drawn. Later inspection resulted in rejection of six of these
on the grounds of pre-1960 LC card dates, leaving 288 titles
in the sample, or 3.1 percent of the universe.

Comparison of Wilson and LC Subject Headings

The Library of Congress and Wilson subject headings assigned to each book were compared and a preliminary categorization was made, as follows:

A. Headings proper identical, subdivided as:
   1. Entire headings were the same, including subdivision if any
   2. LC used subdivision; Wilson did not
   3. Wilson used subdivision; LC did not
   4. LC and Wilson used different subdivisions
   5. LC used a narrower subdivision than Wilson

B. Headings not identical, but covering same subject

C. LC headings narrower than Wilson

D. Wilson headings narrower than LC

E. Headings not comparable
   1. LC heading not matched by a Wilson heading
   2. Wilson heading not matched by an LC heading

Headings were compared individually in all but a very few cases. That is, a single Wilson heading was matched to a single LC heading for the same title, whenever one covering the same subject was available. The preliminary tabulation showed that two special subgroups were important: in a high proportion of headings in category A2 above, the subdivision used by LC was Juvenile literature or Juvenile fiction. A high proportion of the extra headings assigned by Wilson (E2) were either subjects subdivided Fiction or Stories, or form headings such as Short stories or Mystery and detective stories.

Table 5 shows the comparison of headings by title. Categories A1-A5 each contained only a few members; they were therefore lumped together. The number of mixed categories A and E was high enough to warrant separate listing.

The hypothesis is evidently confirmed by this tabulation: the Library of Congress assigned narrower headings than Wilson to only 3.1 percent of the titles in the sample. However, more than one category was applicable to nearly a quarter of the titles (plus more than 10 percent mixed A and E). There-fore, the individual heading comparisons were tabulated (Table 6).

The category in Table 6 which bears on the hypothesis is that of LC headings which were narrower than the com-parable Wilson headings. There were only twenty-two pairs of these (representing twenty-two book titles) or 5.8 percent of the sample. Table 7 lists these headings.

In two of these cases, Wilson uses a single more general heading to cover the same scope for which LC uses two or three headings (Europe, Eastern; Mushrooms). It is quite possible that Wilson's practice is better in these cases. In two more, Wilson has used two general headings where LC has used a single narrower one. These are Atomic weapons and disarmament; and Animals, Air transporation of - Juvenile literature. In the latter case the second Wilson heading is Aeronautics, Commercial, not listed here. In view of the amount of material that would accumulate under the four Wilson headings even in a small library, the LC solution is probably better; the quality of the headings actual-ly used by LC is, of course, another matter.

The next five headings in the table consist of the same first word in each case, but LC uses an adjectival inversion. The Sears list does not provide for inversions for these headings. Actually, each of these inversions is analogous to a subdivision; only the form is different.

TABLE 5:   Comparison of Library of Congress and Wilson
            subject headings, by title

	No. of titles	% of total
All headings identical, [a] including subdivisions[b]	73	25.3
All headings identical, different subdivisions	53	18.4
LC assigned no headings; Wilson assigned at least one[c]	45	15.6
Identical headings, with additional ones assigned by Wilson[c]	32	11.1
LC and Wilson headings use different wording, but cover precisely the same subject	6	2.1
Subtotal	209	72.5
LC headings narrower than Wilson headings	9	3.1
LC headings broader than Wilson headings	3	1.0
Titles to which more than one category applied	67	23.3
Total	288	99.9

a.   Headings were considered identical if the only
variations were in spelling or, in the case of a personal
name, in use or non-use of birth or death dates.

b.   This category includes 20 titles to which no
subject headings were assigned.

c.   For 38 and 6 titles, respectively, the additional
Wilson headings were for fiction or stories. They were
either subjects subdivided by Fiction or Stories, or such
class headings as Short stories and Science fiction.

TABLE 6:   Comparison of Library of Congress and Wilson
           subject headings, by individual headings

	No. of headings[a]	% of total
I. Each LC heading matched to a Wilson heading		
Identical, including subdivisions, if present	122 (244)	32.2
Identical heading; LC used subdivision, Juvenile literature, etc., Wilson did not	47 (94)	12.4
Identical heading; LC used other subdivision, Wilson used none	31 (62)	8.2
Identical heading; Wilson used subdivision, LC did not	3 (6)	0.8
Identical heading; LC and Wilson used different subdivisions	16 (32)	4.2
Identical heading; LC used narrower subdivision than Wilson	11 (22)	2.9
LC and Wilson headings comparable[b]	14 (28)	3.7
Subtotal	244 (488)	64.4
LC heading narrower than Wilson	22 (48)	6.1
LC heading broader than Wilson	5 (10)	1.3
Subtotal	271 (546)	71.8
II. LC and Wilson headings not matched		
LC and Wilson headings covering approximately the same subject[c]	55	7.3
LC headings not in any way comparable to Wilson headings	33	4.4
Wilson headings applied to fiction, etc.	64	8.5
Wilson applies general class headings to non-fiction	27	3.6

	No. of headings[a]	% of total
Wilson headings not in any way comparable with LC headings	32	4.2
Subtotal	211	27.0
Total	757	99.8

a. Part I involves matched pairs of headings (Library of Congress and Wilson); the first number represents the number of pairs. The number in parentheses is a doubling of the first number, to correspond with the numbers in Part II which do not represent matched pairs, except for the category of Library of Congress headings narrower than Wilson. Here, one heading from one service sometimes covers the same area as two or more from the other. Therefore the number in parentheses represents the actual total of LC and Wilson headings.

b. For example: LC, Microbiology; Wilson, Micro-organisms.

c. For example: LC, Teachers - Correspondence, reminiscences, etc.; Wilson, Teaching.

TABLE 7:   Library of Congress headings narrower than
            Wilson headings

LC heading	Wilson heading
Czechoslovak Republic - Descr. & trav. - 1945- Hungary - Descr. & trav. - 1945 - Poland - Descr. & trav. - 1945-	Europe, Eastern
Mushrooms, Edible - U. S. Mushrooms, Poisonous - U. S.	Mushrooms
Animals, Air transportation of - Juvenile literature	Animals
Atomic weapons and disarmament	Disarmament Atomic warfare
Animals, Infancy of - Juvenile literature	Animals
Art, Romantic	Art - History
Coins, American	Coins
Cookery, American	Cookery
Heredity, Human	Heredity
Tales, Caucasian	Folklore, Caucasian
Tales, Irish	Folklore - Ireland
Tales, Persian	Folklore - Persia
Children's clothing	Clothing and dress
Dwellings - Maintenance and repair [Note: this pair occurs twice]	Building - Repair and re- construction
Fantastic fiction	Short stories
Fiction - 19th century - Hist. & crit.	Literature - Hist. & crit.

LC heading	Wilson heading
Fresh-water biology - Juvenile literature [Note: this pair occurs twice]	Nature study
Government & the press - U.S.	Freedom of information
Sika deer - Legends and stories	Deer - Stories
Tanganyika - Descr. & trav. - Juvenile literature	Africa - Descr. & trav.

The Sears list does not use the heading, Tales; reference is made upward to Folklore.

The remaining eight pairs of headings (ten titles) are simply uses of broader headings by Wilson. This represents less than 3 percent of the headings in the sample, and since it appears, from the titles of the books involved, that the LC headings approximately represent the scope of the book, the advisability of even these few broader Wilson headings is dubious. Thus the hypothesis is in general confirmed: LC and Wilson subject headings applied to the same book are of equal scope.

Other comparisons of Wilson and LC policy are possible from Table 6. Aside from its use of the subdivision Juvenile literature, the Library of Congress uses more subdivision than Wilson: 8.2 percent of cases. Wilson applies headings to fiction, stories, and tales on a much larger scale than does LC: 8.5 percent of cases (but this represents 60.4 percent of the total 106 headings applied to fiction by both Wilson and LC), and applies some general class headings to non-fiction: 3.6 percent. Many of the other variations are evidently no greater than the inconsistency to be expected of catalogers.

Comparison of Alanar DS and LC Headings

This comparison was made solely for illustrative purposes. The sample was limited to 196 of the titles appearing in the preceding sample (used for comparison of LC and Wilson subject headings) for which Alanar DS cataloging was also available. While this procedure may have introduced some bias into the sample, a comparison of Tables 6 and 8 shows that the bias was probably not very important. Since

in the comparison between Wilson and LC headings the head-
ing-by-heading comparison proved to be more useful than the
title-by-title comparison, the former was used exclusively
in this section of the study.

Alanar DS headings show what is probably the influence of the LC and Wilson cataloging used for guidance when
available. Proportionally, a few more Alanar headings than
Wilson headings could not be directly matched with LC headings; however, the 6 percent difference in this category
masks several important differences: only 1.8 percent of
the headings in the Alanar-LC comparison, but 7.3 percent
of those in the Wilson-LC one, were different, but covered
approximately the same subject. Alanar applied, proportionally, 85 percent more headings to fiction and stories
than did Wilson.

In the category of headings which could be matched
directly with LC headings, there are likewise two important
differences. In the Wilson sample, over 80 percent more
headings than in the Alanar sample were identical except for
LC's use of such subdivisions as Juvenile literature. These
headings must be scattered through the other categories in
the Alanar sample, since Alanar does not use the subdivision
Juvenile literature.

Probably due to the influence of LC catalog copy on
Alanar, Wilson applied broader headings than LC to about
55 percent more titles than did Alanar.

In general, Alanar subject cataloging is quite similar
to Wilson's. Since both are intended for approximately the
same audience, this would seem logical.

TABLE 8:   Comparison of Library of Congress and Alanar
subject headings, by individual headings[a]

	No. of headings	% of total
I. Each LC heading matched to an Alanar heading		
Identical, including subdivisions, if present	78 (156)	28.0
Identical heading; LC used subdivision, Juvenile literature, etc., Alanar did not	19 (38)	6.8
Identical heading; LC used other subdivision, Alanar used none	52 (104)	18.6
Identical headings; Alanar used subdivision, LC did not	0	0
Identical heading; LC and Alanar used different subdivisions	7 (14)	2.5
Identical headings; LC used narrower subdivision than Alanar	4 (8)	1.4
LC and Alanar headings comparable	13 (26)	4.7
Subtotal	173 (346)	62.0
LC heading narrower than Alanar	11 (22)	3.9
LC heading broader than Alanar	3 (6)	1.1
Subtotal	187 (374)	67.0
II. LC and Alanar headings not matched		
LC and Alanar headings covering approximately the same subject	10	1.8
LC headings not in any way comparable to Alanar headings	25	4.5
Alanar headings applied to fiction, etc.	88	15.8
Alanar applies general class headings to non-fiction	28	5.0

TABLE 8: continued

	No. of headings	% of total
Alanar headings not in any way comparable with LC headings	33	5.9
Subtotal	184	33.0
Total	558	100.0

a.   The footnotes to Table 6 are applicable here.

Summary

There is no significant difference in the relative scope of the subject headings applied to the same books by two major cataloging services, one intended for small general collections and the other for large research collections. The service which is intended for large collections is more likely to subdivide, or to subdivide more minutely. This conclusion is reminiscent of the discussion in Chapter II, which showed that the number of subdivisions applied is directly correlated with the size of the file under a given heading.

The service intended for smaller collections applies large numbers of form or class headings to fiction. While some at least of these headings might be useful even in larger libraries, their application does not appear to be the result of an established coordinated policy. Some of the headings, if consistently applied, would surely produce large undifferentiated files even in many smaller libraries. Some of them (Mystery and detective stories; Short stories) duplicate shelving categories in most libraries. Often a subject heading subdivided Fiction is applied to a title which is not about the subject; for instance, the name of a country so subdivided is likely to be applied to a book which is simply set in the country.

These extra headings applied to fiction, plus some of the class headings used for nonfiction, may represent an attempt to provide access to material in relation to the subjects included in school curricula. If so, this is probably a highly valuable form of access, but (1) a consistent policy should be devised and publicized for use of these headings;

and/or (2) the possibility that other forms of access, such
as booklists or even a separate card file, might be preferable, should be investigated. At the very least, it should
certainly be possible to distinguish these headings on the
catalog card by some such distinctive feature as brackets.

Notes

1. For example: Margaret Mann, Introduction to Catalog-
    ing and the Classification of Books, 2nd ed., p. 143.
    "... all books treating of psychology could be grouped
    under this term ... in the very small library, but in
    the larger library it will be necessary to consider
    the subject in its many applications."
        Barbara M. Westby, "Preface to the Ninth Edi-
    tion," in Sears List of Subject Headings, 9th ed.,
    p. 6. "Specificity is relative and depends on the
    size of a library, its function, and its patrons."
        Julia Pettee, Subject Headings, p. 80-81. "In
    using the Library of Congress headings it is up to
    each library to decide how far it will go in adopting
    the very specific headings increasingly found in that
    list. Shall the ordinary library scatter its Indians
    by tribal names?..."

2. Eloise Rue and Effie LaPlante, Subject Headings for
    Children's Materials.

3. Sidney L. Jackson, "Sears and Library of Congress
    Subject Headings, Report of a Sample Comparison,"
    Illinois Libraries, XLIV (November, 1962), 608-630.

4. Harold L. Roth, Theodore C. Hines and Martin Colverd,
    Technical Services for the Memphis and Shelby
    County Public Libraries; Report of a Study made for
    the Libraries, p. 12-13.

5. Alanar produces two kinds of printed catalog cards, DS
    (Dewey classification and Sears subject headings), and
    DL (Dewey classification and Library of Congress
    subject headings). The former are analogous to
    Wilson cards--cataloging is abbreviated and annota-
    tions are included; the latter to Library of Congress
    cards. Only the former were used in this study.

Chapter V

Use of Form Headings

Terms applied to bibliographic items in order to describe their form--physical, literary, or publication--are
not, properly speaking, subject headings at all, in the sense
that they do not describe the subject content of the item,
that is, what it is about. However, they are conventionally
regarded and treated as if they were subject headings; and
the confusion in terminology has paralleled a lack of careful
definition in the use of these terms, which are also known
as form headings. Headings of this type could equally well
be applied to works which are in the forms they describe or
to works about these forms; in many cases they are applied
to both without distinction. For instance, the heading Catalan drama theoretically could be used for: (1) works about
Catalan drama; (2) collections of plays in Catalan; and (3)
single plays in the language.[1]
    Cutter defines "form-entry" as "registry under the
name of the kind of literature to which the book belongs."[2]
Haykin defines a form heading as "a heading used for a form
entry in a catalog, e.g., Encyclopedias and dictionaries,
Periodicals, Short stories, sometimes known as 'form subject heading,'" and refers to Cutter's definition.[3]
    The clearest rules for the use of form headings, and
those which form the basis of practice today, are those
given by Cutter. He called for "a form-entry for COLLEC-
TIONS of works in any form of literature,"[4] noting that

112

avoiding multiplication of entries in the catalog was the only
reason for not making form entries for single works in a
particular form.

For "practical form," more commonly known as form
of publication (e.g., encyclopedias and dictionaries), Cutter
recommended indicating the form by an appropriate form
subdivision in all cases. Finally, he recommended form
entry of periodicals either under that term or under the
name of the language followed by "periodicals," e. g.,
English periodicals; French periodicals.

The Vatican Rules call for form headings for "works
which have no definite subject in themselves."[5] These headings are based on form of publication or literary form
(though the latter are used for collections and anthologies
only). Either sort of form heading may be modified by an
adjective indicating the language or political or religious
view of the publication.

Haykin's treatment of form headings is diffuse. He
does state that manuscripts and manuscript facsimiles require the form heading Manuscripts, modified by language
(and subdivided Facsimiles, if appropriate).[6] General atlases are to be brought together under the form heading
Atlases. In his discussion of music subject headings, he
states that the singular form of name for musical forms is
to be used for works about the form, and the plural for
works in the form. Works in a medium (i.e., for a particular instrument or group of instruments) are entered
under the medium. In passing, Haykin also mentions in this
section that the heading Short stories is used for collections
in that form. He says that Encyclopedias and dictionaries,
and Almanacs, are used for individual examples of the kind

of publication, not for books about these forms. [7]

Julia Pettee mentions form headings only from the standpoint of those which might be omitted. She states that for well-known literatures, form headings such as Poetry; Fiction; Literature, Greek; etc., should not be used in research libraries for works of individual authors. Furthermore, "the general form heading Periodicals is quite uncalled for. "[8]

Sears uses, for literary form where both singular and plural are available, the singular for works about, and the plural for collections in, the form. Where there is no true plural, the subdivision Collections is used. For minor literary forms, the heading is used for both collections and individual works, with no subdivision unless the number of books warrants. Collections of biographies, not limited to an area or class of people, are entered under Biography. [9]

A general summary of rules for use of form headings might be: Enter special forms of publication, not limited to a particular subject, under the name of the form. The exception to this rule is periodicals, which should not be entered under the name of the form. Enter collections of literary works by several authors under the name of the literary form, preceded by the name of the language. Include individual works in the minor literary forms, and minor literatures. Enter musical works under the name of the form or the medium.

Of course, the problem is not really so simple. Haykin's guide to application of LC subject headings is quite inadequate where form headings are concerned; yet works in these special literary, publication, and other forms make up a significant part of any library's collections. It would be

useful to learn in more detail just what principles may have
guided use of form headings. One possibility is hinted at in
several discussions: the amount of literature to be found in
the form. Cutter's recommendation of form entry for works
of individual authors in the rarer literatures; Julia Pettee's
remark that libraries were dropping this sort of entry in the
more important literatures; Frick's instructions to enter
under form individual works in minor literary forms--and
without subdivision unless the number of titles warrants; all
lead naturally to the conclusion that the number of titles in
the form may have been a major factor in determination of
policy on form entries.

The hypothesis to be tested in this study was that
application of form headings and headings denoting the type
(e.g., Fiction as a heading for novels) rather than the subject of a work is significantly correlated with the size of the
file that has accumulated or could be anticipated to accumulate under the heading.

In order to test the hypothesis all the headings in the
previously selected 10 percent sample of the LC subject
heading list were examined. Those that might be used to
designate a form or type of work were listed. Roughly,
they may be distributed as follows throughout the LC classification.

A	(polygraphy)	18
B	(religion, psychology)	24
C	(biography, etc.	1
D	(history)	1
G	(recreation)	2
H	(social science)	5
J	(political science)	2
K	(law)	9
M	(music)	221
N	(fine arts)	3

116   Subject Analysis

P (philology and literature)   101
Q (science)   7
T (technology)   3
Z (bibliography)   1
Miscellaneous unclassifiable   2

            Total   400

As might be expected, the form headings are concentrated
in the music and literature classes. Table 9 lists those
headings falling in other classes.

In the discussion that follows, music subject headings
have been treated separately from all other headings. A
special policy has been followed at the Library of Congress
with regard to music. Until 1955 all music was entered in
the shelflist; entries for separate pieces of music were not
made in the card catalog. Since 1955 all music, including
separates, has been entered in the card catalog, but separates are not entered in the shelflist unless they are of
special historical or other interest. Furthermore, comparison of the headings with the classification shows that the
former are used, appropriately enough, to give a different
breakdown from that provided by the latter. Many of the
headings might correspond to several class numbers; a given
heading may share the same class number with several other
headings. While this same situation exists in the case of
some headings other than music, it is not nearly so preva-
lent in other areas.

One remark on the music headings is in order here.
Of the 221 headings, nine are miscellaneous ones that might
reasonably be found in the list (Hobo songs; Playground
music); and eighteen indicate national or ethnic groupings or
are other inverted headings (Music, American; Music,
Jewish). The remaining 194 (almost half of the total sample)

TABLE 9: Possible form headings, not in literature or
                    music classes

    A   (Polygraphy)

        Catalan newspapers
        Catalan periodicals
        English newspapers
        English periodicals
        Finnish newspapers
        Finnish periodicals
        Finnish-American newspapers
        Flemish newspapers
        Flemish periodicals
        Lettish newspapers
        Lettish periodicals
        Mexican newspapers
        Mexican periodicals
        Questions and answers
        Swedish newspapers
        Swedish periodicals
        Swedish-American newspapers
        Swedish-American periodicals

    B   (Religion, psychology)

        Association tests
        Avesta
        Bhagavatas
        Bible. Manuscripts
        Bible. Manuscripts, Coptic, [Greek, Latin, etc.]
        Bible stories
        Bible stories, English, [French, German, etc.]
        Buddhist meditations
        Buddhist sermons
        Christian biography
        Christian literature, Early
        Christian literature, Early (Collections)
        Clerical ability and aptitude tests
        Crusade bulls
        Lenten sermons
        Letters, Papal
        Liturgical dramas
        Liturgies
        Ordination sermons
        Rabbinical literature
        Sacred books

TABLE 9: continued

B   (Religion, psychology) cont.

Sunday-school literature
Thanksgiving day addresses
Vocabulary tests

C   (Biography, etc.)

Obituaries

D   (History)

Pleas of the Crown

G   (Recreation)

Bible games and puzzles
Joropo (Dance)

H   (Social science)

Bills, Legislative
Bills, Private
Insurance surveys
Orders in council
Sunday legislation

J   (Political science)

Chicago.   Charters
Treaties

K   (Law, assumed)

Agrarian laws of Rome
Agricultural laws and legislation
Agricultural laws and legislation (Jewish law)
Agricultural laws and legislation (Mohammedan law)
Agricultural laws and legislation (Roman law)
Agricultural laws and legislation, Colonial
Insurance laws
Judge-made law
Town laws

TABLE 9: continued
    N   (Fine arts)

        Art calendars
        English wit and humor, Pictorial
        Flemish wit and humor, Pictorial

    Q   (Science)

        Botanical literature
        Clebsch-Gordan coefficients

    T   (Technology)

        Casserole receipts
        Lenten menus
        Traverse-tables

    Z   (Bibliography)

        Incipits

    Scattered throughout classification

        Technical reports
        Text-books

are headings for the specific instruments and instrument
groupings (including the voice) which individual musical
works require for their performance; or headings for specific forms, sometimes also followed by designation of instruments used, such as Bourrées (Harpsichord). These headings are listed in Table 10. These headings are not subject
headings; as will later be shown, they are used solely for
collections or individual pieces of music; yet they consume
a great deal of space in the subject heading list. It is
worth considering whether they should perhaps be treated in
the same way as species names, names of individual persons, etc., in that only examples of the type might be given
in the list itself.

TABLE 10:   Music subject headings

Status in official cataloga	Heading
	Bourrées
3	Bourrées (Orchestra)
	Bourrées (Harpsichord)
	Celesta and harpsichord music
2	Celesta music
	Cithern music
1	Cotillions
	Cotillions (Piano)
	English guitar music
2	English horn and flute music
4	English horn and flute with string orchestra
2	English horn and harp music
4	English horn and harp with string orchestra
3	English horn and oboe music
4	English horn and oboe with string orchestra
	English horn and organ music
	English horn and piano music
2	English horn and piano music, Arranged
	English horn and trumpet music
	English horn and trumpet with string orchestra
2	English horn music
	English horn with chamber orchestra
4	English horn with chamber orchestra
4	English horn with orchestra
	English horn with string orchestra
1	Jotas
	Jotas (Orchestra)
1	Kobza music
2	Lyra-viol music
2	Lyre-guitar music
	Lyre-guitar music (2 lyre-guitars)
	Oboe and harp music
	Oboe and harp with string orchestra
	Oboe and harpsichord music
1	Oboe and harpsichord with string orchestra
1	Oboe and organ music
	Oboe and percussion music
	Oboe and piano music
	Oboe and piano music, Arranged

1	Oboe and violin music
1	Oboe and violin with string orchestra
4	Oboe and violin with orchestra
1	Oboe d'amore music
	Oboe d'amore with string orchestra
	Oboe music
	Oboe music (2 oboes)
1-4	Oboe, violin, violoncello with string orchestra
4	Oboe with chamber orchestra
4	Oboe with orchestra
4	Oboe with orchestra, Arranged
	Oboe with string orchestra
4	Oboe with string orchestra, Arranged
	Player-piano music
	Plectral ensembles
1	Sacred duets
4	Sacred duets with chamber orchestra
	Sacred duets with harpsichord
	Sacred duets with instr. ensemble
2	Sacred duets with orchestra
	Sacred duets with organ
	Sacred duets with piano
4	Sacred duets with string orchestra
	Sacred duets with various acc.
	Sacred monologues with music
1	Sacred nonets
1	Sacred octets
	Sacred quartets
	Sacred quartets, Unaccompanied
	Sacred quartets with instr. ensemble
	Sacred quartets with organ
	Sacred quintets
1	Sacred quintets with chamber orchestra
	Sacred quintets with instr. ensemble
1	Sacred quintets with 2 pianos
1	Sacred septets
1	Sacred sextets
	Sacred sextets with chamber orchestra
	Sacred songs
	Sacred songs (High voice) with chamber orchestra
1	Sacred songs (High voice) with harpsichord
	Sacred songs (High voice) with instr. ensemble
2	Sacred songs (High voice) with lute
	Sacred songs (High voice) with orchestra

TABLE 10: continued

Status in official cataloga	Heading		
	Sacred songs	(High voice)	with organ
	Sacred songs	(High voice)	with piano
	Sacred songs	(High voice)	with reed-organ
	Sacred songs	(High voice)	with string orchestra
	Sacred songs	(High voice)	with various acc.
1	Sacred songs	(High voice)	with viol
	Sacred songs orchestra	(Low voice)	with chamber
1	Sacred songs	(Low voice)	with harpsichord
	Sacred songs	(Low voice)	with instr. ensemble
	Sacred songs	(Low voice)	with orchestra
	Sacred songs	(Low voice)	with organ
	Sacred songs	(Low voice)	with piano
	Sacred songs	(Low voice)	with string orchestra
4	Sacred songs	(Medium voice)	with band
4	Sacred songs orchestra	(Medium voice)	with chamber
	Sacred songs	(Medium voice)	with guitar
1	Sacred songs	(Medium voice)	with harpsichord
	Sacred songs ensemble	(Medium voice)	with instr.
	Sacred songs	(Medium voice)	with orchestra
	Sacred songs	(Medium voice)	with organ
	Sacred songs	(Medium voice)	with reed-organ
	Sacred songs, Unaccompanied		
2	Sacred songs with harpsichord		
	Sacred songs with instr. ensemble		
	Sacred songs with organ		
	Sacred songs with piano		
2	Sacred trios		
	Sacred trios, Unaccompanied		
4	Sacred trios with chamber orchestra		
1	Sacred trios with harpsichord		
	Sacred songs	(Medium voice)	with piano
	Sacred trios with organ		
	Sacred trios with piano		
	Sacred vocal music		
2	Trumpet and drum music		
4	Trumpet and drum with band		

	Trumpet and organ music
3	Trumpet and organ music, Arranged
	Trumpet and piano music
	Trumpet and piano music (Jazz)
	Trumpet and piano music, Arranged
1	Trumpet and piano with orchestra
2	Trumpet and piano with string orchestra
	Trumpet-calls
	Trumpet music
	Trumpet music (Jazz)
	Trumpet music (2 trumpets)
	Trumpet music (2 trumpets), Arranged
3	Trumpet with band
4	Trumpet with chamber orchestra
4	Trumpet with dance orchestra
4	Trumpet with orchestra
4	Trumpet with orchestra, Arranged
1	Trumpet with string orchestra
4	Trumpet with string orchestra, Arranged
1-4	Trumpets (2) with orchestra
4	Trumpets (2) with orchestra, Arranged
4	Trumpets (2) with string orchestra
4	Trumpets (3) with band
	Tuba and piano music
	Tuba and piano music, Arranged
	Tuba music
3	Tuba with band
4	Tuba with band, Arranged
2	Tuba with orchestra
2	Vocal duets
	Vocal duets, Unaccompanied
	Vocal duets with chamber orchestra
	Vocal duets with guitar
	Vocal duets with harp
	Vocal duets with harpsichord
	Vocal duets with instr. ensemble
	Vocal duets with lute
	Vocal duets with orchestra
	Vocal duets with piano
4	Vocal duets with string orchestra
	Vocal duets with various acc.
	Vocal ensembles
	Vocal ensembles with orchestra
	Vocal music

TABLE 10: continued

Status in
official
catalog[a]   Heading

	Vocal music, German
	Vocal music, Italian
1	Vocal nonets
1	Vocal octets
	Vocal octets, Unaccompanied
	Vocal octets with orchestra
	Vocal quartets
	Vocal quartets, Unaccompanied
4	Vocal quartets with chamber orchestra
4	Vocal quartets with dance orchestra
	Vocal quartets with instr. ensemble
4	Vocal quartets with orchestra
	Vocal quartets with piano
	Vocal quartets with piano, 4 hands
1	Vocal quintets
	Vocal quintets, Unaccompanied
2	Vocal quintets with instr. ensemble
1	Vocal quintets with organ
1	Vocal septets
	Vocal septets, Unaccompanied
1	Vocal sextets
	Vocal sextets, Unaccompanied
1	Vocal sextets with orchestra
1	Vocal sextets with piano
	Vocal trios
	Vocal trios, Unaccompanied
	Vocal trios with guitar
2	Vocal trios with harpsichord
	Vocal trios with instr. ensemble
	Vocal trios with piano
	Vocal trios with piano (4 hands)
	Vocal trios with 2 pianos

a. The numbers in this column indicate that under this
heading in the LC official catalog:

> 1. No titles have been entered, with or without sub-
> divisions, but there is no note on the authority card to
> indicate why.

> 2. The notation "no material as yet" appears on the
> authority card.

3. The notation "not in LC" appears on the authority card.

4. The notation "not used without subdivisions" appears on the authority card.

If there is no number in this column, there are entries under the heading in the official catalog.

In computing the number of cards under headings in the official catalog and shelflist, the following procedure was adopted: if the file of cards under the unsubdivided heading, or in the class, was less than an inch long, the cards were individually counted and each was inspected to determine if the title was an example of the form under consideration. If the file was more than an inch thick, it was measured with a ruler, and the number of inches multiplied by 100. An approximate figure for proportion of form to subject entries was then determined when necessary. This figure is a rough one: the Information Systems Office at the Library of Congress has sampled the catalogs and indicates that the density varies from eighty-seven to 113 cards to the inch. However, for purposes of the study it was assumed that any file with seventy-five to 100 cards or more was a comparatively large one, and the issue of whether a particular class or heading contained 200 or 225 cards was not significant. The results of the investigation seem to show that the assumption was justified.

Of the 179 non-music headings in the sample, only 97 could be used in the analysis. Of the group analyzed, 88 were used as form headings and were therefore found in the official catalog; appropriate classes in the shelflist containing entries for works in the form were found for 38 of this

group. For only nine headings that were not used for the
form of literature was it possible to get data from the shelflist on the number of titles in the form. Since the range
for this group was from eight titles to twenty-six drawers
of cards, no reliable general conclusion could be drawn.

Of the 82 headings which could not be used in the
analysis, thirteen were shown not to be applied to works in
the form, but data could not be gathered on the number of
titles actually held which were examples of the form in
question. Nine of these were for newspapers in various
languages. (The classification for newspapers has not been
developed at the Library of Congress.) Technical reports
and Text-books would be scattered throughout the entire
classification. Bible stories are unavoidably written in some
language, and the name of the language is always used in the
heading when it is applied to collections of stories. The
heading Sunday-school literature has several class numbers
in the LC list, but other, narrower form headings appear to
be used in all cases where this heading might be applicable.

The remaining sixty-nine unusable headings fall into
a number of groups: literature headings in which the parenthetical specifications (Collections) and (Selections: extracts,
etc.) are used for collections in the form; headings under
which no example of the form appears, and for which either
no class number could be determined or where there was no
material in the class; and headings such as Tell-el-Amarna
tablets where items in the form would be entered under the
heading as main or added entry. LC policy of course pro-
hibits double entry of the latter items.

Since significant results, positive or negative, were
not possible on the basis of the hypothesis, the headings

were studied from the point of view of the kind of form involved. Here more meaningful conclusions are possible.

The grouping used follows the main classes of the Library of Congress classification appropriate to the headings to a certain extent, but not entirely. As each group is discussed, its relation to the LC classification will be shown.

Literary Forms

In headings for forms of literature, practice varies according to both form and language. Single works in most forms and languages are not entered under the form heading. For purposes of this study, the headings expressing a literary form are divided into three subgroups: (1) those preceded by an adjectival specification of language or national origin; (2) religious literary forms; (3) other, minor forms. The first and last would fall almost entirely into class P of the LC classification; the second group would fall largely into the B class, although a few would be classifiable as P.

1. Literary forms preceded by adjectival specification of language or national origin. --Treatment of these forms varies with the importance of the language and with that of the form. The distinction between major and minor forms and languages is empirical. In major forms in major languages only collections by several authors are entered under the form heading, and for these collections the heading is always followed by either (Collections) or (Selections: extracts, etc.). Minor forms are those to which the parenthetical specifications is never applied, even in major languages; minor languages are those to which the parenthetical specification is never applied, even for major forms.

In major languages only collections by several authors receive the form heading, and for these collections the heading is always followed by either (Collections) or (Selections: extracts, etc.). The major forms of literature by this definition are as follows:

> Literature
> Drama
> Fiction
> Poetry
> Prose literature

However, the last of these is borderline in its classification. It occurs four times in the sample; all four languages are major by the definition used, but parenthetical qualification is used only for English prose literature. The other three languages include only one or two entries each in the form.

The major languages or national specifications occurring in the sample are:

> Catalan
> English
> Flemish
> Mexican
> Swedish

The major language classification is somewhat fluid. The parenthetical specifications are not used for prose literature in Flemish, Mexican or Swedish; or for drama in Catalan or Swedish; and the evidence is that their use for Flemish poetry is recent.

The distinction between major and minor forms as a function of the number of titles in all languages in a given form is not completely clear cut: the range for the major forms is from 38 to 1,442 titles in the official catalog, while the range for minor forms is from 2 to 380 titles.

The distinction between major and minor languages in the major forms, however, is very clear. When the total

number of titles using a major form as a form heading in
the official catalog is found for each language, the range is
from 46 to ca. 2,371 titles[10] in the major languages, and
from zero to 23 titles in the minor languages. Table 11
shows the total number of titles in these forms in the official catalog, in all languages in the sample. This distinction holds despite a policy followed by the investigator in the
case of obscure languages such as Kechua and Lettish (Lat-
vian) where it was not possible to determine from dictionaries whether the title of a given item indicated that the
book was about the form or was an example of it. This
policy was to include all questionable titles in the tabulation
with a note to the effect that the two types might be mixed
in the count. Thus the counts for minor languages almost
certainly include a few titles in which the heading was
actually used as a subject heading. There is, therefore,
probably an even greater difference between the number of
titles in the major and in the minor languages than the tabu-
lations show. This problem did not arise with the major
languages: the investigator was able to read titles in three
of the five; the key words in the remaining two were learned
rapidly.

Minor forms and minor languages present a different
picture. In this case, also, only collections receive the
form heading, but it is applied without modification, so that
examples of the form and works about it are not distinguished
in the catalog. It would seem that no matter how "minor"
the form or language, titles in and about the form should be
distinguished in some way; otherwise two kinds of concepts
are intermingled. Furthermore, the number of titles entered under a minor form is not always small; for example,

TABLE 11:   Major literary forms

Heading	No. of form entries in official catalog
I. Major languages	
Catalan	70
English	ca. 2371
Flemish	46
Mexican	100
Swedish	49
II. Minor languages	
Albanian	0
Assyro-Babylonian	9
Cebu	0
Celtic	0
Celtic (English)	3
Finnish	23
Finnish (Swedish)	9
Hittite	3
Kashmiri	0
Kazakh	0
Kechua	8
Lettish	14
Swedish-American	5
Tatar	0
Telugu	0

about 238 entries appear in the official catalog under the
heading English wit and humor. Probably some of these entries are subject rather than form; yet the searcher must
sort through all the cards to find them. Examples of a form
and works about it are conceptually different, and should be
distinguished in the catalog in all cases. The parenthetical
subdivisions (Collections) and (Selections: extracts, etc.)
cause filing problems; in current filing practice they precede
subdivisions using the dash, while all other parenthetical
modifiers follow. One reasonable possibility might be to re-
serve the unmodified heading for collections of materials in
the form, and to make use of the subdivision History and
criticism (or some other appropriate subdivision) for works
about the form. There is a precedent for this suggestion in
the heading English literature, which does not appear in the
official catalog without subdivision.

2. Religious literary forms. --There are nineteen headings
in this group. They show a different pattern from non-religious forms. Most of these headings would fall in LC class
B, but a few are classified in P. In general these headings,
listed in Table 12, are used for both collections and individual works, with the exceptions noted below. (Certain
headings, where there are few entries, are assumed to
cover individual works, even if none appear.)

Bible stories includes no form entries: the stories
themselves are unavoidably in some language and inverted
headings indicating the language are used. The treatment
here is notably different from that of Science fiction, where
English language collections are entered directly under the
heading without further specification. English language collections of Bible stories are entered under Bible stories,

TABLE 12: Religious literary forms

Heading		No. of form entries in official catalog
Bible plays	ca.	100
Bible stories		0
Bible stories, English	ca.	300
Bible stories, French		5
Bible stories, German		35
Buddhist meditations		4
Buddhist sermons		4
Christian literature, Early		0
Christian literature, Early (Collections) [and (Selections: Extracts, etc.)]	ca.	137
Christian poetry, Early		2
Lenten sermons	ca.	175
Letters, Papal		1
Liturgical dramas		18
Liturgies		76
Liturgies, Early Christian	ca.	30-40
Ordination sermons	ca.	112
Rabbinical literature (Collections) [and (Selections: Extracts, etc.)]		25
Sunday-school literature		1
Thanksgiving Day addresses	ca.	125

English. Christian literature, Early and Rabbinical literature use the parenthetical specifications (Collections) and
(Selections: extracts, etc.) for collections; individual works
are not entered under the form heading.

Sunday-school literature is evidently not used as a
form heading despite the class number given in the LC subject heading list. All the entries under this number in the
shelflist which show evidence of assignment of any subject
headings use other, usually narrower, headings. The one
entry in the official catalog under Sunday-school literature
(Collections) is dated 1892, so it is safe to say this entry
does not represent a policy in force today.

3. Other non-religious literary forms.--This group includes
twenty-six headings, listed, together with the number of entries in the form found in the official catalog, in Table 13.
These headings include special kinds of the major forms
(Lyric poetry); and forms less important than those receiving
national or linguistic specification, where this specification
is either omitted or placed after the name of the form (In-
vective; Maxims, French). Inspection of these headings
brought out evidence of inconsistencies with the subject heading list in a number of cases. The scope note for Lyric
poetry indicates that only collections not limited to a particular country are entered under the heading. However, of the
thirty-one entries under this heading, many are limited to
the lyric poetry of a particular country. It seems reasonable to guess that many catalogers have not been content
with the alternative offered by the scope note: that collections of the lyric poetry of a particular country are entered
under the national adjective followed by poetry (English
poetry; French poetry). That is, established policy offers

TABLE 13: Other literary forms

Heading	No. of form entries in official catalog
Alexandrine verse	0
Bathetic poetry	1
Curiosa	1
Decimas	2
Drolls	5
Ghost plays	1
Ghost stories	ca. 112
Invective	6
Joruri	1
Lays	4
Letters	34
Lyric poetry	ca. 31
Maxims	ca. 362
Maxims, Buddhist	1
Maxims, French	6
Maxims, Oriental	4
Nō (Japanese drama & theater)	0
Nō plays [used for texts]	1
Prologues and epilogues	12
Quatrains	0
Quatrains, Dutch	0
Revolutionary poetry	4
Revolutionary poetry, Chinese	1
Revolutionary poetry, Georgian	0

no means of specifying the lyric poetry of a particular country.

Nō (Japanese drama and theater) is used only for works about this art form; texts of the plays themselves are entered under Nō plays--a heading added since the closing date of the seventh edition of the subject heading list.

The authority card for the heading Quatrains contains the notation "no material in catalog." It was probably established to complete the structure, since Quatrains, followed by a national or linguistic adjective, is used (but, as it happens, only for works about the quatrain as a form).

Finally, the unmodified heading Science fiction is used for English-language collections, although no scope note to this effect is provided, and a similar practice is not followed with respect to other headings.

These twenty-six headings, when applied to forms of literature, are used, so far as could be determined, solely for collections. In few instances in this group was there available a class number even reasonably coextensive with the heading; therefore, it was not possible to test what follows. Most of the headings are for forms in which the individual work is likely to be relatively brief; therefore the application of these headings to collections only may be as much due to literary warrant as to any policy decision. The sole exception is Science fiction, where there would be many separate works: enough to justify a decision to enter only collections.

Periodicals and Newspapers

Headings consisting of a linguistic adjective followed by newspapers or periodicals are used only as subject headings, not as forms. These headings would be in class A; seventeen occurred in the sample.

Headings used as Main or Added Entry for Works in Form

The eight headings in this group could not be considered because LC policy would preclude their use as form entries. This policy is that of not repeating the same item as both main (or added) and subject entry. These headings are:

> Avesta
> Bible. Manuscripts
> Bible. Manuscripts, Coptic, [Greek, Latin, etc.]
> Chicago. Charters
> Gesta Romanorum
> Tell-el-Amarna tablets

Law

The thirteen headings in this category would fall into class K (Law), or H or J in some cases. In no case was the unsubdivided heading used for individual laws or compilations of legislation, although in some cases compilations were entered under the heading subdivided geographically. In only two cases were class numbers available, and in one of these cases (Agricultural laws and legislation), compilations were entered under the heading subdivided geographically, while in the other (Sunday legislation) the available numbers were scattered according to the particular topic (labor, mails, etc.) so that a count in the shelflist would not have revealed anything. In the remaining cases, listed below, no determination of the number of entries in the form was possible with the procedure used.

> Agrarian laws of Rome
> Agricultural laws and legislation (Jewish law)

Agricultural laws and legislation (Mohammedan
law)
Agricultural laws and legislation (Roman law)
Agricultural laws and legislation, Colonial
Bills, Legislative
Bills, Private
Insurance laws, International
Judge-made law
Ordinances, Municipal
Town laws

Science and Technology

The universe of headings in this group is much too
small (ten items) to permit statistical treatment, but the relation between length of file and use as form headings is
clear, nonetheless. All the headings appear in the Q and T
classes. One heading, Science news, cannot be compared,
as it is not used for the form, and no class number is
available for the form either. But of the remaining nine
headings, seven are used as form headings and two are not.
The former have from one to about 100 entries in the official catalog; the latter have 13 1/4 inches and 26 drawers of
entries, respectively, in the shelflist. Of course, these
numbers, for Genetic literature and Botanical literature, respectively, do not really indicate much: most of the items
in the shelflist would be on much narrower subjects. What
is revealing is that science and technology headings are in
general used as form headings. The seven thus used in the
sample are noted below:

Casserole receipts
Clebsch-Gordan coefficients
Lenten menus
Planispheres
Plant lore
Plant names, Popular
Traverse-tables

Miscellaneous

    There are twenty headings remaining. No real cate-
gorization is possible; the policies followed vary. A tabulation is presented in Table 14.

Music

    The headings in Class M are of three major types,
as described previously. Of the nine headings in the miscellaneous groups, all but two: Music, and Playground
music, are used as form headings. The heading Music is
so broad that to use it as a form heading would be impossible, while Playground music may be just the reverse:
there are only two subject entries under this heading in the
official catalog, and it is perfectly possible that the Library
of Congress owns no titles to which this might be applied as
a form heading. The other headings each have only a few
form entries in the official catalog as shown below.

Alabados	2
Graduals (Music)	13
Hobo songs	1
Music calendars	19
Music title-pages	11
Psalms (Music) ca.	200
State songs	1

    The eighteen inverted music headings are in general
used for examples of the form. Of the seven of these headings for which it was not possible to find evidence of use for
the form, most either contain few or no subject entries, or
are headings for kinds of music for which there may be no
titles in the form, such as Music, Assyro-Babylonian. The
headings in this group are listed below with, in the case of
those used as form headings, the number of form entries in
the official catalog.

TABLE 14: Miscellaneous form headings

                                     No. of form entries
                                     in official catalog

Works in form entered under heading
   followed by (Collections) or
   (Selections: extracts, etc.):

Sacred books   37
Treaties   ca.   200

Used as form heading:

Art calendars   7
Bible games and puzzles   30
Christian biography   ca.   250
Clerical ability and aptitude tests   1
Crusade bulls   1
Incipits   4
Pleas of the crown   34
Questions and answers   ca.   150
Vocabulary tests   2

Not used as form heading:

Association tests
Bhagavatas
Insurance surveys
Joropo (Dance)
Orders in council
Technical reports
Text-books

No entries in official catalog; no class
   number available:

Obituaries
Synonyms

Headings used for the form:

Music, African	6
Music, American	11
Music, Czech	1
Music, Ethiopic	2
Music, French	3
Music, Hindu	11
Music, Incidental	ca. 100
Music, Jewish	10
Music, Oriental	3
Music, Popular (Songs, etc.)	71
Music, Primitive	80

Headings not used for the form:

Music, Assyro-Babylonian
Music, Baroque
Music, Brazilian
Music, Byzantine
Music, German
Music, Greek and Roman
Music, Polynesian

The music headings in the third and largest category --those for specific instruments and forms of music--all follow the same general pattern with variations. All are used as headings for the form only; some, particularly those for specific instruments and combinations of instruments, are used only with subdivisions. Others have been established without regard to literary warrant; that is, there are no entries under the heading in the official catalog and the authority card contains the notation "no material as yet." While some of these headings were evidently established to produce a full structure of headings for a given instrument, others do not show evidence of this reasoning. Thus the headings in the left column below each contain the notation "no material as yet," while there are entries under the corresponding headings in the right column.

English horn and flute	English horn and flute with
music	string orchestra
English horn and harp	English horn and harp with
music	string orchestra

On the other hand Celesta music is the only subject heading for this instrument, and it also contains the "no material as yet" notation. This notation appeared on authority cards for eighteen of the 194 headings in this group; four others contained the probably similar notation "not in LC." In addition, there are a number of other headings for which no entries at all, or only an authority card, were found. Since the reasons for this circumstance might vary--withdrawal of the last item under the heading, or cards misplaced in the file--attaching any importance to the number of headings in the list but not recorded in the official catalog might be misleading.

However, if it is LC policy not to use certain music headings without subdivision, surely a note to this effect should appear in the subject heading list. Furthermore, as was mentioned previously, the inclusion in the subject heading list of the many headings for specific instruments and instrument combinations, a significant proportion of which have never been used, is open to question. The same purpose might be served by treating these headings in the way that personal, species and place names are treated: inclusion in the list of examples, and of those headings for which special cross referencing is required. Table 10 lists the 194 headings in this group and designates each one that contains the notations "no material as yet," "not in LC," or "not used without subdivision," or for which no entries, subdivided or not, were found.

Original Plan of Investigation

The original plan was to examine the entries under
the possible form headings in the Library of Congress Catalog of Books: Subjects, to determine if they were actually
used as form rather than subject headings, and then to measure the number of titles actually in the forms in the LC
shelflist. This course was adopted because it was under-
stood that the card catalogs at the Library of Congress contained cards under form headings that were not recommended
for other libraries (by tracings on the cards) because
LC's stacks were closed. Much later this was discovered
to be a false impression, at least so far as the official
catalog was concerned.

Meanwhile, search of the printed LC subject catalog
revealed the need for a number of refinements in the method.
It became evident that almost everything that could be entered under a form heading was so entered in this tool: for
example, every quinquennial cumulation contains several
pages of Tamil fiction entries, nearly all evidently single
novels. However, in most cases the titles listed under these
headings do not bear the heading as a tracing in the Library
of Congress Catalog of Books: Authors. Therefore, the entries under the headings in the subject catalog were examined;
several of those in each form were checked in the author
catalog. A heading was not considered to be used as a form
heading unless entries found under it were both (1) examples
of the form; and (2) traced for the heading in the author
catalog.

A further refinement was required because many headings might be used to indicate form in situations where it
was impossible to judge, due to the nature of the literature,

that this was the case. This applied primarily to Art headings. Even if the books themselves were examined, it
would not be possible to judge if a heading was applied on
the basis of the reproductions of art works present in a
book or the text about these reproductions which almost always accompanies them.

For this reason, only those headings which could be
judged to have been applied (or not to have been applied) on
the basis of the actual form of work were considered meaningful for the purposes of the study. On this basis, eighty-
two headings were rejected from the initial sample. Of
these, fifty-one began with the word, Art, and twenty-seven
began with either Inscriptions or Cuneiform inscriptions.
The remainder were Cuneiform writing, Fire-marks, Graf-
fiti and Mezzotints. In the case of all these headings, it
is evident that the only items on which a judgment could with
confidence be based would be portfolios of reproduction with
no commentary whatsoever: these are probably numerically
unimportant in the universe of real, as opposed to conceivable, publications.

A further group of twenty-four headings was rejected
from the sample because experience with the subject catalog
and at the Library of Congress made it apparent that, while
these headings were not used as form headings, this was
almost certainly due to the nonexistence of actual titles in
the form (e.g., a simple collection of marriage proposals
sounds highly unlikely). These headings are listed below:

Aggregates	Bills of health
Airworthiness certificates	Bills of particu-
Bible (a scope note indicates	lars
that this heading is used	Bills of peace
only with subdivision)	Circular letters

Insurance policies   Marks of origin
Inversions (Geometry)   Marriage licenses
Judgment notes   Marriage proposals
Judgments (seven   Questionnaires
   headings)   Schedules, School
Magic squares

The eleven headings beginning with the word **Propa-**
ganda were rejected because use of these for forms would
involve a moral judgment on the work involved.

There were twelve headings which, if used as form
headings, would apply to individual works. It is possible to
debate whether a heading of this type would be a form heading. At any rate, only one, **Marriage of the King's Son**
(Parable), is so used, and the three such entries in the official catalog are for films. The other headings are for the
names of individual treaties, laws, and tests; it is possible
that lack of literary warrant is the reason for lack of form
entry under these headings. Since in no case was there an
LC class number available specifically for copies of the individual item, it was impossible to check this possibility.
The headings, classifiable mainly in B, D and E, are listed
below:

Anti-Comintern Pact
Arras, Treaty of, 1485
Magna Carta
Mills bill
Ordinance of 1787
Tree test
Tua test
Warsaw Pact, 1955
Wartegg-Biedma test
Wartegg test
Wartegg-Vetter test

The final major problem arising at this stage of the
investigation was that of dealing with headings for forms of

music (Vocal duets; Sacred songs; etc.) which do not actually
appear in the printed subject catalog, except in very rare
instances.

Of course, a number of other headings in the sample
did not appear in the printed subject catalog. Since the
catalog was not begun until 1950, this result was to be expected.

It was not possible to draw a firm conclusion about
many of the headings from the subject catalog: only if there
was an actual form entry under the heading was it possible
to check the author catalog to see if the item was traced
from the form. The results of the investigation of the card
catalogs at the Library of Congress were far more significant. No conclusions would have been possible on the basis
of the headings tested in the Catalog of Books: Subjects;
therefore the results of this part of the study were not sub-
jected to further analysis.

On investigation at the Library of Congress, it was
determined that the policy on form headings in the official
catalog was not as previously believed. The entries under
these form headings were traced on the printed cards; there
were no files under headings like English poetry, such as
those which appear in the printed subject catalog. The original plan was therefore modified. The number of cards
under the sample headings in the official catalog was calculated and the use (or non-use) of these headings for form of
work in the official catalog was adopted as the required
indicator.

Summary

Although current practice cannot be described precisely by a brief statement, most headings that could be applied to forms of material are so applied except for the very broadest ones. Headings for forms of literature are applied only to collections, and where larger amounts of material appear, the parenthetical expressions (Collections) and (Selections: extracts, etc.) are usually applied. Headings for musical forms and for instruments required by a type of music are used for collections and individual works, although often only with subdivisions. Other music form headings are generally used for collections in the form.

Most science and technology headings are applied to the form: the collection vs. individual works question is not prone to arise here.

Headings for newspapers and periodicals (the only form-of-publication headings in the sample) are not used for the forms; neither are headings for laws and legislation.

Notes

1. The use of form subdivision of actual subjects (e.g., English language - Dictionaries) is somewhat better defined than the conditions under which main headings are applied to forms. This part of the investigation is limited to the latter.

2. Cutter, Rules, 4th ed., p. 21.

3. Haykin, Subject Headings, p. 101.

4. Cutter, Rules, 4th ed., p. 81-82.

5. Vatican Library, Rules, 2nd ed., p. 309-310.

6. Haykin, Subject Headings, p. 64.

7. Ibid., p. 78-79.

8. Pettee, Subject Headings, p. 91-92.

9. Bertha M. Frick, "Suggestions for the Beginner in
    Subject Heading Work, " in Sears List of Subject
    Headings, 9th ed. , p. 14-29.

10. In counting headings, those inverted headings given in
    the list as examples of national or linguistic distinc-
    tions (e.g. , Science fiction, French, [Russian, etc.];
    Manuscripts, Coptic, [Greek, Latin, etc.]) were
    counted as two or three headings.

Chapter VI

Styling of Subject Headings for
Computer Arrangement[1]

All library catalogs of any significant size suffer
from problems of arrangement. The main effect of the use
of computers to arrange catalog entries has simply been to
make the problems more evident. The general solution for
manual filing in library catalogs has been to compile rules
for filing which required consideration of the semantic content of the entry by the filer (and then by the searcher).
For instance, a distinction is often made between the same
word(s) designating a person, a place, a thing or a title.
This solution has worked after a fashion, but its inadequacy
has been clear for some time.

The use of computers to arrange catalog entries has
made the problem more complex. The computer cannot distinguish, for instance, between a person and a place on the
basis of the characters in the entry alone. A human filer
can distinguish Washington, George, from Washington, D. C.
because he already knows that the former is our first presi-
dent and the latter is a city. The only way to enable a
computer to make the same distinction is to devise, and
key, a set of codes that explicitly defines these characteristics. To make and code the many distinctions required
for the computer to sort entries into the order used by a
library would probably require somewhat more effort on the
part of human beings than would simply sorting the entries

by hand. Furthermore, even if it were feasible to computer-
sort catalog entries into a conventional library order, to do
so without questioning the need for such complexity would
not be wise. The rekeying of a catalog into a new form
presents perhaps the best opportunity in several generations
to bring entry form and filing arrangement into harmony with
present and anticipated needs.

While there have been a few studies of the problem
of computer filing, most of these have not looked at the
problem from both points of view: that is, they have not
first questioned the need for complex, non-alphabetical
arrangements and then attempted to devise procedures for
computer filing on the basis of conclusions as to what was
really needed. For instance, the study by Nugent[2] assumed
the LC filing rules as a base and attempted to devise keying
and formatting procedures to implement them on the computer. The result is extremely complex and no basis for belief that this complexity is worth the cost of achieving it is
ever offered.

While descriptions of them frequently do not appear
in the published literature, many of the earlier computer-
produced book catalogs have gone to the opposite extreme of
simplification, very likely from necessity. Entries and filing
arrangements have been radically simplified to fit the requirements of standard computer sorts. While this solution
is usually adequate for small book-form catalogs, larger
ones do require some refinements.

The Library of Congress is now involved in a study
of filing rules as a complement to the Marc project.[3] This
investigation is in its early phases.

Basis of this study

At least one study has attempted to examine the problems of computer filing in terms of the principle that filing should, insofar as possible, be a mechanical process, whether performed manually or by machines.[4] This implies that filing should be based on the characters appearing in the entry, not on judgments about the entry or the meaning of groups of characters appearing in it. The justification for this principle is not the needs of computers, but rather the fact that any judgment made by the filer must also be made by the person attempting to find entries in the file. For this reason it seemed best to keep arrangement as simple as possible. This filing code concentrated on author and title entries, because it became obvious very early in the study that subject headings required far more analysis than it was feasible to give them at the time. It was this filing study which provided the framework for the study of subject heading styling described in this chapter.

The present study took as its hypothesis that styling of subject headings can be effected in such a way as to make feasible a consistent and meaningful computer arrangement using (for arrangement) only the characters appearing in the entry. Only styling as such was considered; for instance, no attempt was made to determine if a given inverted heading (or all inverted headings, for that matter) should preferably be entered directly. In all cases the entry word was not changed; in fact, no changes were made up to the first punctuation mark in a heading.

The object was to change headings to file in accordance with the filing rules of Hines and Harris[5] (called "the

computer filing code" below), in which the characters
space, letters A-Z and numerals 0-9 are filed on in that
order, and all other characters are ignored. Sub-elements
in filing elements are designated by two spaces, producing
a sub-element by sub-element sort automatically; for instance:

> Michigan - History
> Michigan algorithm decoder

There are certain requirements for the styling of subject headings for computer arrangement by the computer
filing code. Full use of punctuation without interfering with
the sort routine is necessary. Furthermore, some of the
sub-arrangements currently in use (such as chronological,
place and inverted) might serve a useful purpose; it should
be possible to retain any that do. Many subject headings,
specifically personal and place names, are already provided
for in the computer filing code. All provisions of the code
that apply to these headings must be included in the styling
process.

Finally, styling of anything--subject headings included
--requires a set of rules. It was further assumed that so
long as the purpose was accomplished, the simpler the rules
the better. It was realized very early that an explicit set
of rules to produce useful unambiguous headings by the styling procedure every time would require a highly trained
person to apply them. Since most existing headings would
require no change, and since the number of kinds of change
required in the vast majority of the remaining headings was
very small, the skill of the highly trained person would be
wasted most of the time. Furthermore, no matter how
highly skilled the styler, the headings produced would have

to be edited to correct errors and omissions. Therefore,
the procedure was devised as a two-step one. First, simple
rules for styling would be applied clerically. The results
of this process would be computer-sorted, and then edited
both for errors and for that small proportion which did not
emerge from the styling as useful headings.

Before a set of rules for subject heading styling
could be developed, the dimensions of the problem had to be
established, in terms of the provisions of the computer filing
code used as a basis, and the possible areas of conflict in
the present form of subject headings. A brief description
of the important points of the filing code provides the former; a survey of subject headings was necessary to provide
the latter.

Arrangement under the computer filing code is, as in
all library practice, first by entry. Within entry, arrangement is by field. Examples of fields are author, subject
heading, added entry, and title. The code suggests but does
not require that a field be defined by three spaces after it.
A field is often divided into subfields, defined by two spaces.
In this case, arrangement within the field will be by subfield. Within subfields, arrangement is by word. A word
is defined as a set of characters with a space before and
after it. Arrangement is letter by letter within each word,
according to the following order of sorts: space, letters of
the Roman alphabet A-Z, Arabic numerals 0-9. Modified
letters are set equal to their unmodified equivalents; upper-
case letters equal lower-case letters.[6] Numbers are filed
as numbers, not as isolated digits, e.g., 19 comes after 2.

All other characters, including punctuation, are completely ignored for sorting purposes. They are not treated

as spaces. Thus, U.S. does not equal U. S. If no space
is put between the period and the S, it will file as US.

The two preceding paragraphs are basically another
way of writing Rule 1 of the American Library Association
(ALA) filing rules, first edition, [7] which were in force when
the computer filing code was written. With one addition
also present in the code, this is likewise a summary of the
first three basic rules of the ALA filing rules, second edition. [8] This addition is the stipulation that modified letters
are treated as their unmodified equivalents, and that capitals
and lower-case letters are to be filed the same. The fourth
basic rule--ignoring of initial articles--is covered by a
more general provision of the computer filing code: that an
entry must be arranged on the characters appearing in it,
and that any character(s) to be ignored in filing should not
appear in the entry. This provision, incidentally, is in accord with the basic principle of the new edition of the ALA
rules: "Filing should be straightforward...not disregarding
or transposing any of the elements..."[9]

The computer filing code provides for three optional
special non-printing symbols which would not be ignored in
arrangement. These symbols are intended primarily for use
with proper nouns or adjectives, where usage may require
printed characters different from the characters arranged on.
An example is Van Allen, which is typically arranged as
VanAllen. This example shows a possible use of one of the
symbols: that which indicates a space in the printout, but
which is ignored in filing. The second is the reverse: it
is filed as a space, but is not so printed out. This one
might be used if it were thought essential to arrange hyphenated compound words as two words. The last symbol

indicates elements to be ignored in filing.

All these symbols are optional; on the principle of illustrating the worst case, none was used in the subject heading styling study. Thus, the arrangement produced uses the simplest available punching conventions, and is as "bad" as any such arrangement would be. It is then possible to decide if the symbols would be of significant value in subject headings.

One other specific provision of the computer filing code which enters the problem of subject headings is corporate body and place arrangement. Corporate bodies always have two spaces between each part of the name to indicate subfields: U.S. Department of State. Office of the Secretary. Files. Institutions entered under place have only one space after the place name: New York. Stock Exchange. It should be noted, however, that an institution entered under place may then have a part of its organizational hierarchy indicated by two spaces: Chicago. University. Libraries. This arrangement accords with the ALA filing rules, first edition, and with the LC filing rules, [10] but not with the new edition of the ALA rules. The last provides for strict word-by-word filing, and interfiles corporate bodies and institutions entered under place. This alternative makes sense; it can be accommodated under the computer filing code simply by insuring that the same number of spaces appear in both cases. Most of the present study was performed before this new edition was published, and corporate and place entries appeared only rarely in the universe of subject headings used. Therefore the study was completed under the old rules which in this case are the more complex and difficult.

Problems presented by subject headings in their present form

The other side of the problem, the relation of the present form of subject headings to the computer filing code, required a preliminary study. Certain limitations were assumed, all arising out of the fact that styling as such was all that was done. To take an inverted heading as an example, the comma might be changed to a dash producing a heading-subdivision combination, or the inversion might be made a parenthetical expression, but the order of the inversion would not be reversed to make the heading direct. The latter type of change involves many other factors than filing, and requires further study.

Aside from place and name headings, which are provided for by the computer filing code, the main problems in subject headings arise from the use of punctuation as an implicit filing element. There is no way to computer-arrange subject headings according to either the LC or the old ALA filing rules without keying special symbols to indicate the type of heading. For instance, the comma is filed on in some subject headings. The sequence ", " (comma space) sometimes (when it is used in an inverted heading) has a filing position between the sequences " (" (space left parenthesis) and " [any alphameric character]". When the comma sets off members of a series it is ignored. And sometimes there are two files of inversions--ethnic, cultural or linquistic; and all others. There is no way to program these distinctions without keying special symbols.

The new ALA filing rules, on the other hand, interfile word-by-word all entries with the exception of personal surnames. They thus blur the distinctions which the various marks of punctuation are intended to show. There is no

reliable evidence that one filing arrangement is better than
another; it is highly possible that some of the previous distinctions are worth keeping.   At any rate, the form of subject headings over the years has become so complex that a
rationalization would be an improvement, regardless of the
filing rules used.

A preliminary study was made to determine what
kinds of conflicts there were between the present filing order
of subject headings and the way they would file under the
computer filing code.   For the purpose, a 10 percent sample
of the headings in the sixth edition of the LC subject heading
list was taken by arbitrarily starting on page seven and re-
viewing all the headings (including see references) on that
page and on every tenth page thereafter.   All marks of
punctuation occurring were listed, classed by the punctuation
mark used and by the type of heading and purpose for which
it was used.

Where a given heading and its subdivisions were not
complete on the sample page, this heading was reviewed in
its entirety over as many pages as it covered.   Thus, all
the U.S. headings were checked.   In addition, all the headings for William Shakespeare and New York were checked,
in order to be sure that the problem of personal and place
names with complex subdivisions was adequately covered.

The sample was not taken for statistical purposes.
No frequency counts were made at this stage.   A 10 percent
sample, plus the additions mentioned, was thought to be adequate to assure a high likelihood that all significant complexities in heading form were covered.   This supposition
was borne out.   After page 500 (less than halfway through
the list), very few new complexities were found.

Sub-arrangements in the LC List

In addition to the count, examples of the most complex entry groupings were selected, and from these groupings the following list was compiled. This list agrees in essentials with the LC filing rules; but it is a composite in that in no case have all eight sub-arrangements been found to occur under the same heading.

1. Heading without subdivision.
2. Heading with topical and form subdivisions set off by a dash.
3. Heading with period subdivisions set off by a dash, and filed chronologically.
4. Heading with national, ethnic, cultural, or special subdivisions (usually separated only when there are many subdivisions under the heading).
5. Heading showing part of an organizational hierarchy, set off by a period.
6. Heading followed by a qualification in parentheses.
7. Heading with an inversion, set off by a comma.
8. Heading with national, ethnic, or cultural inversion (usually separated only when there are many such inversions).
9. Phrase heading beginning with the same word(s) as 1-8 above.

As headings are presently written, the computer alphabeting code arranges the groups above as follows:

1. Heading without subdivision.
2. Two, four, five, and those headings in three above in which the period subdivision begins with alphabetic characters, interfiled.
3. The remainder of three above, arranged chronologically.
4. Six through nine above, interfiled.

This listing assumes a typical keying convention: a
space on either side of the dash, two spaces following the
period, one space before the left parenthesis, and one after
the comma.

Punctuation Changes Proposed

The following types of punctuation are used in LC
subject headings: apostrophe, double quotes, colon, hyphen,
parentheses, comma, period and dash.

Colon

Only one use of the colon was discovered. The
parenthetical expressions (Collections) and (Selections: extracts, etc.) are used on LC printed cards, with literature
headings, both general and national. These headings have
never appeared in the printed list, with the single exception
of the heading Christian literature, Early (Collections). The
general heading, since the second edition of the LC list,
has been Literature - Collections, with a see reference
from Literature - Selections. Both of these are arranged in
the alphabetical sequence with the other subdivisions set off
by the dash. The parentheses in this case are used as a
device to arrange these headings before all other subdivisions, even though this provision requires an exception to
the general rule that parenthetical expressions file after subdivisions using the dash.

At any rate, the only occurrence of the colon in LC
subject headings is in a subheading that has not been offi-
cially recognized in the subject heading list. Also, the filing
in this case can be perfectly straight-forward; there is no
arrangement problem with the colon. Therefore, this study
need make no provision for headings containing a colon.

Apostrophe and double quote

The apostrophe, double quote, and hyphen are used in LC subject headings only as they would occur in words, not as a part of subject heading grammar. The apostrophe is used to denote the possessive case and in certain foreign names. Artists' marks, in any library catalog, is always arranged as Artists marks; it would also arrange that way on the computer. The same applies to the name D'Orsay. The double quote is used as quotation marks and causes no problem.

Hyphen

The hyphen is used in four ways in the LC list: to connect two usually independent entities--Argentine-Brazilian War, 1825-1828; in hyphenated compound words or names; in words with hyphenated prefixes--Anti-Aircraft; and in inclusive dates.

Words with hyphenated prefixes are filed as single words under most filing rules in use today. They will so file on the computer, with no special provision required. The hyphen in inclusive dates is likewise not a problem as such. The dates are the filing element in these cases, and filing is on the first date of the pair, followed by the second date. (However, see the discussion of dates, below, for the problem of two periods both beginning with the same date, but with one of longer duration than the other.)

The two remaining uses of the hyphen do present problems that must be dealt with in any rules for alphabetizing of subject headings. Compound words and independent entities connected by the hyphen (both usually filed as two words) will file as a single word on the computer. Examples are:

Library of Congress Arrangement	Computer Filing Code Arrangement
Argentine ant	Argentine ant
Argentine ballads and songs	Argentine ballads and
Argentine-Brazilian War,	songs
1825-1828	Argentine carols
Argentine carols	Argentine drama
Argentine drama	Argentine essays
Argentine essays	Argentine farces
Argentine farces	Argentine literature
Argentine literature	Argentine newspapers
Argentine newspapers	Argentine periodicals
Argentine periodicals	Argentine poetry
Argentine poetry	Argentine Republic
Argentine Republic	Argentine rummy
Argentine rummy	Argentine-Brazilian
Argentines	War, 1825-1828
	Argentines
Lead	Lead
Lead alloys	Lead alloys
Lead-antimony alloys	Lead arsenate
Lead arsenate	Lead bronze
Lead bronze	Lead burning
Lead burning	Lead compounds
Lead compounds	Lead in the body
Lead-copper alloys	Lead industry and trade
Lead in the body	Lead mines and mining
Lead industry and trade	Lead ores
Lead-lithium alloys	Lead plating
Lead mines and mining	Lead tree
Lead ores	Lead-antimony alloys
Lead plating	Lead-copper alloys
Lead-poisoning	Leadership
Lead tree	Lead-lithium alloys
Lead-work	Lead-poisoning
Leadership	Lead-work
Leaf catalogs	Leaf catalogs
Leaf hoppers	Leaf plants
Leaf-miners	Leaf rust of wheat
Leaf-mold	Leaf-hoppers
Leaf plants	Leaflets
Leaf-rollers	Leaflets dropped from
Leaf rust of wheat	aircraft
Leaf-spot	Leaf-miners

Leaflets	Leaf-mold
Leaflets dropped from aircraft	Leaf-rollers
	Leaf-spot
League of Cambrai, 1508	League of Cambrai, 1508

If desired, the optional symbol discussed previously may be used to make two entities connected by the hyphen arrange as two words. This symbol is the one that is treated as a space for arranging purposes, but appears neither as a symbol nor as a space in the printout.

Hyphenated compound words are a major problem as the LC subject headings are currently written. The Century Dictionary was used as an authority.[11] This produced far more hyphenation than is warranted by current usage, and any project for modernization of the list would require the use of a more up-to-date authority for spelling of compound words.

Parentheses

According to Daily the parentheses are used for three purposes: "To explain confusing or synonymous terms...to disperse headings which would otherwise be grouped together as in the numerous headings with the word 'Law,' in some form, in parentheses; and to group headings together as in the series beginning 'Cookery (Apples)'..."[12] Daily excludes from this listing the many headings with parentheses for musical instruments or musical compositions: Concertos (Bassoon, clarinet, trumpet). However, this is a form of grouping analogous to the Cookery headings. In another case, the parenthetical expression, while belonging to the first of Daily's three groups, actually substitutes for a scope note: France - History - Revolution - Language (New words, slang, etc.).

Another use of the parentheses may be seen in the example Apes (in religion, folklore, etc.), where the parentheses are used as a device to prevent this heading from filing among the phrase headings. However, the same structure is used without the parentheses in other headings. Devon, Eng., in literature is an example.

Parentheses are used throughout the LC subject heading list to produce an inversion within a subdivision: France - Relations (general) with the U.S. Another type of use of parentheses, not specifically discussed by Daily, is to explain a phrase subheading referring to a period of time, by putting dates after it: English Language - Middle English (1100-1500). These headings are intended to file chronologically.

A more useful categorization of parenthetical expressions for filing purposes would be the following. Note that some might overlap.

1. To define an obscure or ambiguous expression or a homograph.

2. To show what aspect of a subject is treated.

3. To set off a prepositional phrase.

4. To set off dates.

5. To set off an inversion within a subdivision.

6. To specify instrument or instrument grouping in music headings.

7. To specify a system of law in legal headings.

None of the headings in the LC list which include parenthetical expressions are filed in strict word-by-word order. However, that is how they would file on the computer as they are presently written. Mass (Chemistry) would arrange as Mass chemistry among the phrase headings.

Comma

The comma is used in the LC list for a number of
purposes which fall naturally into two main groups: inversions of various types, and uses as a punctuation mark exactly as it would be used in ordinary text. Inversions are
used for two main purposes: as a means of subject subdivision, different from dashed topical subdivisions only in
that (usually) an adjective is used instead of a noun (Acids,
Fatty; Cookery, American; Concertos (Violin), Arranged).
(But note that the direct form of this last heading--Arranged
concertos (Violin)--is not of a sort that would appear in
text.) The comma is also used to bring the main word forward for arranging purposes, as in personal and place
names: Shakespeare, William; Africa, Central; and in such
entries as Ackia, Battle of, 1736.

Incidentally, the use of the comma, because it would
occur in ordinary text using the same groupings of words,
runs the full gamut of possibilities. There are commas in
series (Bassoon, clarinet, flute, horn, oboe with orchestra);
commas in place names (Arvin, Calif; Devon, Eng., in
literature); commas used to set off dates (Barrier treaty,
1709); and commas used in corporate names (Methodist
Episcopal Church, South). An interesting sidelight is that
this last heading is filed in the LC list as though the comma
represented an inversion.

The two main uses of the comma discussed above
present different problems. The use in ordinary punctuation
can generally be permitted to stand. In fact, it must be,
because any punctuation of this type could easily appear in
a title entry, and the computer filing code holds revision of
titles from appearance on the title page to a minimum. In

addition, the comma in these cases is not arranged on in
any filing rules, so the arrangement produced by the computer filing rules would not change the normal order.

However, inversions now are usually arranged in a
separate file, following both subdivisions using the dash and
parenthetical expressions, but preceding phrase headings.
Under the computer alphabeting code inversions will interfile
with phrase headings: Acids, Fatty arranges as Acids fatty.

Inversions using the comma in personal names cause
no problem. Inverted geographical names may be interfiled
with some phrase headings, but no significant problems
should occur, and it is recommended that they too be left
as they are.

Period

As is the case with the comma, periods have a dual
function in subject headings: as marks of ordinary punctuation and as a cataloger's device. The period is used in
abbreviations: Salvage (Waste, etc.), which causes no
difficulty.

Use of the period in subject headings as a cataloger's
device is in accordance with the author entry rules. The
period, just as in author entry, is used to set off the subdivisions of a political hierarchy (France. Armée), in form
entries (Catholic Church. Liturgy and ritual), and in entry
under place (New York. Stock Exchange).

The computer filing code provides for the period in
these cases: in the first two it is followed by two spaces,
producing a subfield; in the third it is followed by only one
space, so that a straight word-by-word arrangement results.
Thus, New York. Stock Exchange will interfile with phrase
headings beginning with New York, contrary to the old (but

not the new) ALA and the LC filing rules but in accordance
with the trend toward stricter alphabetical arrangement in
many libraries today.   Likewise, form entries and subdivisions of political hierarchies, since they are made subfields,
will interfile with subdivisions using the dash.

Thus, no uses of the period in subject headings will
require specific provision beyond that already made in the
computer alphabeting code.

Dash

The dash occurs extensively in subject headings.
Strictly speaking, it is used for one purpose only--to subdivide a subject by means of a noun or noun phrase. However, it is in subdivisions using the dash that the greatest
arranging complexities of all appear in the LC list and in
present catalogs.   Daily has shown "that subject subdivisions
differ from main headings only in the character of the typo-
graphy used to list them." When a noun modifies another
noun, but cannot be used in a phrase or inversion, it is
put after the main heading, with a dash between.[13]

However, the arrangement of subdivisions set off by
the dash is quite complex when any significant number of
entries is involved.   The order of entries with dashed subdivisions in the LC list is as follows:

1. Subject without subdivision.

2. Subject with form and general aspect sub-
    divisions.

3. Subject with time subdivisions, arranged
    chronologically.

4. Subject with special subdivisions.

5. Subject with geographical or place subdivisions.

The special subdivisions (group 4 above) need some explanation. The device of separate arrangement of so-called special subdivisions is resorted to in the subject heading list as a classificatory device to separate one type of heading from other types. Examples are national, religious, and ethnic author subdivisions under national literatures (English literature - Catholic authors) and names of types of animals as subdivisions under parts of the body (Cardiovascular system - Mammals). The old ALA filing rules (pages 56-59) provide a subject arrangement based on the LC list and following the order given above, with the addition of other forms of subject heading (those not using the dash). However, the LC filing rules (pages 140-149) make no provision for separation of special subdivisions from form and subject subdivisions.

The computer filing code requires that there be a space on either side of the dash, so that subdivisions are treated as subfields. All dashed subdivisions are then interfiled, except that in the case of time subdivisions, which are intended to file chronologically, dates are required to be provided in all cases, and to be written at the beginning of the subdivision. Since numbers follow letters in the sort routine, time subdivisions therefore arrange in chronological order after the other dashed subdivisions.

It must be admitted that interfiling all dashed subdivisions will produce longer alphabetical files. However, this is really an advantage. There is only one alphabetical arrangement into which cards must be merged, and only one in which they must be found. It is not the length of a file that really produces filing and finding difficulty, but rather its complexity.

Speaking of complexity, it should be noted that Daily has shown that in the LC list, choice of parentheses, inversion, dashed subdivision, or a prepositional phrase for use in a given situation is not usually determined by necessity, but rather by "the skill and experience of the cataloger in evaluating the composition of the list in which he finds it and the necessity of fitting in a new heading."[14]

LC catalogers over the years have not enjoyed unalloyed success in this endeavor. The arrangement of the headings is usually consistent with the LC filing rules. However, as mentioned above, these rules make no provision for the separate arrangement of special subdivisions which often occurs in the subject heading list.

One case of really extreme inconsistency was found. There is a long file of phrase headings beginning with Negroes in..., subdivided into two files: one of various subjects, ranging from Negroes in aeronautics to Negroes in poetry, and one of geographic locations. The analogy here is obvious--to a person studying the subject heading list itself. The rationale would be that these headings are analogous to dashed geographical subdivisions which are always filed after other subdivisions, and that therefore it is reasonable to divide the file in this way. But how about the user suddenly confronted with this sub-arrangement in a catalog?

The tendency in the LC list has evidently been, whenever a grouping of headings beginning with the same word(s) grew rather long, to separate out, by some device or other (often punctuation), some group of headings into a classed sub-arrangement.

Another arrangement, never given in the filing rules

but evident in the list, is that in certain entries where a
number appears as other than the first element, a mental
inversion is made. Piano music (2 hands) files between
Piano music (Boogie woogie) and Piano music (Jazz). This
is demonstrated in the group of entries in Table 15 under
Piano music.

The LC list arrangements are not always internally
consistent, even when the same form of punctuation is used.
For instance, under Artists, all inversions are interfiled,
while under Authors, national inversions are placed in a
separate subfile. In headings beginning with Cookery, all
inversions are interfiled.

These are just a few examples of inconsistencies in
the LC list. There are more, but it would be pointless to
enumerate them. These examples are given only to show
that the list has suffered from lack of overall planning and
supervision, and from acceptance of ad hoc arrangements to
suit particular cases. Systematization is needed, and this
study is intended to make a beginning in that direction.

Summary of punctuation changes proposed

To summarize, the following marks of punctuation
require consideration of styling problems for computer arrangement.

1. Hyphenated compound words. Their spelling
   must be verified in a modern source, preferably the second edition of Webster's Unabridged
   Dictionary.

2. Separate entities connected by a hyphen.
   Either a non-printing symbol indicating a space
   in filing must be keyed, or the two words
   must be allowed to file as one. The latter
   alternative was selected for this study.

3. Parenthetical expressions. The purpose (of

TABLE 15: Piano music headings

Piano music
Piano music - Analysis, appreciation
Piano music - Analytical guides
Piano music - Bibliography
Piano music - Bibliography - Catalogs
Piano music - Bibliography - Graded lists
Piano music - History and criticism
Piano music - Instructive editions
Piano music - Interpretation (Phrasing, dynamics,
Piano music - Simplified editions   etc.)
Piano music - Teaching pieces
Piano music - Teaching pieces - Juvenile
Piano music - To 1800
Piano music - To 1800 - Simplified editions
Piano music (Boogie woogie)
Piano music (Boogie woogie) - Teaching pieces
Piano music (1 hand)
Piano music (1 hand), Arranged
Piano music (2 hands)
Piano music (3 hands)
Piano music (4 hands)
Piano music (4 hands) - To 1800
Piano music (4 hands), Arranged
Piano music (4 hands), Arranged - To 1800
Piano music (5 hands)
Piano music (6 hands)
Piano music (6 hands), Arranged
Piano music (Jazz)
Piano music (2 pianos)
Piano music (2 pianos), Arranged
Piano music (2 pianos, 6 hands)
Piano music (2 pianos, 8 hands)
Piano music (2 pianos, 8 hands), Arranged
Piano music (3 pianos)
Piano music (3 pianos), Arranged
Piano music (4 pianos)
Piano music (4 pianos), Arranged
Piano music (5 pianos)
Piano music (Solovox registration)
Piano music, Arranged
Piano music, Arranged (Jazz)
Piano music, Juvenile
Piano music, Juvenile - Teaching pieces
Piano music, Juvenile (3 hands)
Piano music, Juvenile (4 hands)
Piano music, Juvenile (6 hands)
Piano music, Juvenile (2 pianos)

the five listed below) must determine the
treatment of the heading. Parenthetical expressions are typically used in ordinary language for clarification. Alternatives are
available for the other four uses of parentheses. Styling based on the type of heading
is to be preferred.

a) If the parenthetical expression is used to
define or elucidate the term it should be re-
tained, with the proviso that all uses of such
terms must be followed by a parenthetical expression. Interfiling of dashed subdivisions
with parenthetical expressions will thus be
avoided. The expression should be treated as
a subfield, that is, preceded by two spaces.

b) Where an aspect of the subject is shown
or a classed grouping is produced, the phrase
is made into a subdivision using the dash.

c) By analogy with exactly similar headings,
the parentheses around a prepositional phrase
may simply be removed to produce a phrase
heading.

d) If the parentheses are used to set off dates
in a subdivision which is intended to be arranged chronologically, the dates are moved to
the beginning of the subdivision, and set off
from the remainder by a comma, producing a
result similar to other chronological subdivisions, as described in 6 below.

e) In the few cases where the parentheses set
off an inversion within a subdivision they are
changed to commas, showing the inversion to
be what it actually is.

4.   Inversions using the comma. In all cases the
inversion is changed to a subdivision using the
dash. Furthermore, the preposition at the end
of an inverted prepositional phrase is to be
dropped.

Other changes proposed

        The following provisions repeat parts of the computer
filing code.

5. In headings in which the period is used to set off parts of an organizational hierarchy, sacred book, etc., the period is to be followed by two spaces.

6. Any subdivision which is intended to be arranged chronologically must contain dates as the first element of the subdivision. Any date encompassing more than a single year must consist of the beginning and ending years of the period, for instance, such headings as: Gt. Brit. - History - To 1066 are changed to include a beginning date.

7. All numerals are written as provided in the computer filing code. Roman numerals in filing positions are changed to Arabic. Subelements of filing elements are written in the order in which they are to be arranged.

8. Abbreviations of import in filing are written out; initials intended to file as such have spaces between them. For purposes of the study the former was taken to mean all abbreviations except "etc." With regard to initialisms, the computer filing code provides that acronyms usually pronounced as words be filed as words.

9. To all place names a location designation is to be added if it is not already present.

10. Names with separable prefixes must be written without a space between prefix and name.

Coding for Changes

The 10 percent sample of the seventh edition of the LC subject headings which was used for other parts of the study was used here also. Since these headings were being keyed into machine-readable form for other parts of the study, a method was devised for coding the headings for the styling changes required. These codes were assigned as described below, and keypunched as part of the heading. A

program was written to make most of the changes automatically, punching new cards for these and all unchanged
headings, and to list and label all the headings for which
human intervention was required.

The criteria for styling were taught to a clerk.   The
coding used consisted of a single number or a number and
a letter which the clerk then assigned to those headings in
the sample to which they applied.   The investigator did the
same and afterward compared the results to produce a coded
copy of the subject heading list for keypunching.   Table 16
lists the total number of headings in each category (this
count was produced by the computer program).   Table 17
gives a summary of Table 16 and also shows the number of
errors found in comparison of clerical and professional styling of the list.   Hyphenated compound words are omitted
from Table 17 because the instruction relating to them was
not applied by the clerk at all, and by the time this omis-
sion was evident it would have biased the results.

Analysis of Coding Errors

The table, while it represents largely the clerical
errors detected in editing, also includes a few instances
(about 10 percent of all errors) where the clerk's choice
was judged to be best, or where the editing process resulted
in choice of a third alternative.

A similar analysis, breaking the work into three
sections, showed that practice produced no significant improvement.   Those of the instructions which were adequately
defined and simple to apply (such as those relating to inversions) showed a consistently low error rate.   Those which were
more complicated, particularly those involving parenthetical expressions, showed a higher rate.

TABLE 16: Number of occurrences of each style change

Type of styling	No. of headings
Hyphenated compound words	333
Changes involving parenthetical expressions	
Parenthetical expressions made subfields	276
Parenthetical expressions added	52
Parentheses changed to dashes	236
Parentheses removed from prep. phrases	16
Dates in parentheses moved to beginning of subdivisions	9
Parentheses in subdivisions changed to commas	7
Changes involving inversions	
Inversions changed to dashed subdivisions (without removal of preposition)	917
Inversions changed to dashed subdivisions and trailing prepositions removed	205
Chronological subdivisions requiring addition or relocation of dates	75
Other changes	
Parts of org. hierarchies, etc., made subfields	6
Roman num. made Arabic, and order of subelements changed, if necessary	7
Abbreviations or num. written out	25
Initialisms requiring that spaces be added	44
Place names requiring addition of location designations	3
Names with separable prefixes	3
Total number of changes	2214
Headings with changes marked	2071
Headings not changed	7510
Total sample	9581

TABLE 17:   Number of styling errors, by major types of
            change, found in pre-keypunching edit

Type of change	No. of changes	No. of errors	% errors of total changes
Parenthetical expressions	662	273	41
Inversions	1146	144	13
Dates	102	114[a]	112[a]
Other	69	31	45
Total	1979	562	28

a.   The errors involving dates include a large number (59) which were marked as changes, but should not have
been.   Many headings and subdivisions include dates as iden-
tifiers, not as filing elements, but the distinction is often
not clear to some people.

Dates

        The error rate on dates was high partly because of
the large number of non-chronological headings so marked,
and partly because of failure to mark those which should
have been.   Most chronological subdivisions occur at the
third level, e.g., U.S. - History - Civil War, and tend to
be isolated; they thus are missed.

        The tendency erroneously to mark headings for modi-
fication on the basis of dates could be curbed by identifying
more explicitly the kinds of headings involved, through adding the following to the instructions:

        Many headings and subdivisions contain dates intended
        not as filing elements but as identifiers.   These head-
        ings should not be changed.   Main headings are never
        arranged chronologically.   A few subdivisions are;
        these are nearly always set off from other subdivisions
        of the main heading by a row of asterisks.   Arrange-
        ment by date is most frequently used in sub-subdivisions.

Such subdivisions as History and Politics and government very often are subdivided chronologically.

Parenthetical expressions

    The worst problem by far is that of headings contain-
ing (or requiring) parenthetical expressions. With the exception perhaps of prepositional phrases and dates in parentheses, the choices are not well-defined. The proportion of
errors shows this: nearly half of all the errors made
occurred in this group, although it contained only about a
third of the headings. Here, also, was where the investigator found the most difficulty. In nearly all other cases
the problem is one of picking out the heading which requires
editing; once it is found the decision is straightforward.
Such is not the case with parenthetical expressions. Here
a decision as to the intent of the parentheses must be made.
In some cases it is clear. For instance, in the heading
Addicere (The word) the purpose is obviously clarification
of the way in which the term is being used. In the long
sequence of headings under Cookery, the group of parenthetical expressions is just as obviously used to set off a
special group of subdivisions. On the other hand, the sequence of headings

        Acceleration (Mechanics)
        Acceleration (Physiology)
        Acceleration, Negative
            See Acceleration (Mechanics)

is not so simple. The cross references under Acceleration
(Physiology) are:

        sa Human centrifuge
        Space medicine
        Stress (Physiology)

making it quite plain that the scope of this heading is the

physiological <u>effect</u> of mechanical acceleration. This meaning would be better expressed by a heading such as the
following, of a type frequently occurring in the Library of
Congress list:

> Acceleration, Physiological effect of

This sort of change, however, is beyond the scope of
this study. This heading is intended only as an example,
and a relatively minor one at that, of the problems encountered.

There is even more complexity present. Since the
rules used provide that if a term is used with a parenthetical expression, all occurrences of the term must be so
modified, attention to the headings preceding and following
those modified by parentheses is necessary. Thus, in the
example above, if the decision were that the parenthetical
modification should be kept, simple treatment of the next
heading, <u>Acceleration, Negative</u>, as an inversion would mean
that it would be changed to a heading-subdivision combination
without parentheses. Instead the expression must be provided. Similarly, the sequence

> Akkadians
> Akkadians (Sumerians)
> See Sumerians

requires that a parenthetical expression be added to the first
heading of the pair.

In order to add the proper modification to the heading
above, some knowledge is required (aided here by a scope
note stating the Sumerians were non-Semitic and therefore
implying that the Akkadians were Semitic). The next sequence requires some subject knowledge before determination

can be made as to whether parenthetical modification or
dashed subdivision is to be preferred.

> Batak
> Batak (Palawan)
> Batak (Sumatra)
> See Batak

In cases such as this an encyclopedia was consulted (the
Britannica by preference) for help.

One of the most common parenthetical modifications
was (Law), or systems of law, e.g. (Canon law), (Mohammedan law), (Roman-Dutch law). These modifications occurred sometimes with the only use(s) of the modified term.
In other instances the term also occurred without parenthetical or other modification, as the first word(s) of an inversion, or with parenthetical modification(s) not relating to
law.

This description shows the magnitude of the problem.
It is also an important one since these headings constituted
nearly 7 percent of the total sample, and just under a third
of the headings in which styling changes were made. The
study did not resolve the problem, but did produce further
guidelines for the choice between parenthetical modification
and subdivision by means of the dash. These are listed
below.

1. If the term appears only once in the list, and
   includes a parenthetical modification in that
   use, it is reasonable to assume the modification is intended to explain the use of the
   term in some way; therefore it may be left
   as is.

2. If a term appears only with parenthetical
   modifications denoting systems of law, these
   may be made subdivisions of the term on the
   ground that in this case it is not being explained, but rather that different aspects of
   the same legal term are being shown.

3. In most other modifications of a term by the
name of a system of law, a dashed subdivision is also used, with one exception. Where
the only legal modification is the term (Law),
and the term is also used in a distinctly
non-legal sense, the parenthetical modification is used. In many of these cases of
mixed form, judgment of a relatively high
level is required.

4. In other multiple uses of the term, inspection of the parenthetical modification(s)
(and of cross references, class number,
scope note, and/or subdivisions for any uses
not so modified) demonstrates immediately
that the uses are homographs or fall into
different broad subject areas. While some
caution is required here, in general the
parenthetical modification may be left or
added as the case may be. An example
follows.

Mass (Catholic Church, BX2230-2233)
Mass (Canon law)   (BX1939. M23)
Mass (Chemistry)
  See Atomic mass
Mass (Music)
Mass (Nuclear physics)
  See Atomic mass
Mass (Physics)
Mass, Standards of
  See Standards of mass

Most, if not all, of these headings (with the
exception of the inverted one) involve different meanings of the word Mass, but they are
broadly classifiable into two groups: a
ritual of the Catholic Church, and the mass
of physical substances. These two groups
are homographs, and would definitely require
parenthetical modification. Within the two
groups, the question of subdivision versus
modification remains open, however. When
this kind of problem arose, a solution that
seemed reasonable was selected, sometimes
somewhat arbitrarily.

5. In all other uses of parenthetical modification, judgment must be exercised.

Miscellaneous errors

The error rate for other changes is high because there are so many different types, each occurring quite rarely. This group, if the headings in an actual catalog were being styled, would form a far higher proportion of the total, and the error rate would probably go down.

Changes Made or Identified by Computer

After the headings were coded and punched, they were run through the computer program which made those styling changes that were feasible mechanically and then listed those that were not. Table 18 groups the changes into the two categories. Fewer than 30 percent of the styling changes had to be printed out for human analysis, and of these 414, or precisely 60 percent, were hyphenated compound words which would simply be looked up in a dictionary.

It should be noted that if the entire list, or all the subject headings in an existing catalog, were being styled, certain of the headings which were printed out for human intervention could also have been styled automatically. They were not because the size of the universe did not warrant the programming which would be necessary. Entry of the desired form of perhaps fifteen or twenty of the most common hyphenated words into a dictionary could have eliminated a substantial proportion of these. For instance, the term folk-lore appeared fourteen times in the sample (and was missed, as it happened, several more times in all the coding and editing).

All the subdivisions involving dates could have been checked to see if a date appeared in an acceptable form, and if so, the date could have been moved to become the first

TABLE 18: Styling changes, grouped by ability of the
computer to make them

	Number	Percent
I. Changes not made by the computer		
Hyphenated compound words	333	
Parenthetical expressions added	52	
Dates in parentheses moved to beginning of subdivisions	9	
Chronological subdivisions requiring addition or relocation of dates	75	
Roman numerals made Arabic, and order of subelements changed, if necessary	7	
Abbreviations or numbers written out	25	
Initialisms requiring that spaces be added	44	
Place names requiring addition of location designations	3	
Names with separable prefixes	3	
Subtotal	551	25
II. Changes made by the computer		
Parenthetical expressions made subfields	276	
Parentheses changed to dashes	236	
Parens. removed from prep. phrases	16	
Parens. in subdivisions changed to commas	7	
All inversions	1122	
Parts of org. hierarchies, etc., made subfields	6	
Subtotal	1663	75
Total	2214	100

element in the subdivision. In over half of these headings
(56) the date was already present.

There are few Roman numerals in the list; a dictionary could have provided for translation of these to Arabic
numerals, and their relocation if necessary. Nearly all
initialisms are the first "word" in a heading; most of these
could have had spaces added automatically, and since a
separable prefix is nearly always the first word of a subject
heading, the space between it and the rest of the name could
be removed automatically.

In the last two instances, however, it would be advisable to print out the modified heading for human confir-
mation that the spaces had been removed or added in the
right place.

The computer punched new cards for the automatically
styled headings so that the changes and additions could be
made easily. These cards were edited at this stage and
typographical errors not caught previously, plus the few occasions where the styling changes had not been made correctly by the computer, were corrected. Once the program
was thoroughly debugged there were very few of the latter.

The headings for which styling changes were not to
be made automatically were printed out for human intervention, with an indication of the problem involved in each one.

A policy was adopted for dealing with these terms
and for others such as complicated groups of parenthetical
expressions. This policy was in keeping with the purpose of
the study, which was to test the feasibility of the procedure
proposed, not to produce subject headings for 10 percent of
the list which could be taken over and used as they stood.
Where material had to be supplied, the most obvious depend-

able source (usually the Encyclopaedia Britannica) was accepted as a reasonable approximation. Any hyphenated
compound word which was not found in Webster's Unabridged Dictionary was left hyphenated and not searched
further. If this proposed procedure were to be applied to
the whole subject heading list for actual library use, the
usual searching procedure would have to be followed to
verify all these headings. This step was not necessary for
this study.

For the same reason (the limited purpose of the
study) the headings referred to in see references were not
styled. The actual headings referred to by the see references would in most cases not appear in the sample and
would therefore not be styled. Any styling of all subject
headings in the list would have to include see references.

Procedure for Headings Printed Out for Manual Styling

The headings containing hyphenated compound words
were turned over to a clerk, with instructions to look each
one up in the second edition of Webster's Unabridged Dictionary. Table 19 shows the results of this analysis. If
the headings which were not found in Webster are not taken
into account, the following proportions result:

Hyphenation kept	29 percent
Made two words	54 percent
Made one word	17 percent

Thus, for 71 percent of the verifiable hyphenated
compound words in the sample (57 percent of all the hyphenated compound words in the entire sample), the spelling in
the Library of Congress list is out of date.

In 40 percent of cases (those left hyphenated) the

filing of these terms might vary from that to be expected by the usual rule that hyphenated compound words are filed as though they were two words. This rule is, however, a convention, and the opposite should be just as acceptable.

TABLE 19: Analysis of hyphenated compound words

Action taken	Number	Percent
Hyphenation kept	80	24
Made two words	145	43
Made one word	45	13
Not found in Webster	67	20
Total	337[a]	100

a. The number 333 previously used represents the number of headings containg compound words; this number is the total number of compound words--a few headings contained two.

The sixty-seven terms which were not found in Webster's dictionary were nearly all either foreign or specialized technical terms. Due to the searching and judgment of sources that would have been required, these words were left hyphenated in accordance with the policy set forth above.

The remainder of the headings which were not automatically styled (218 in all), involved a great many types of changes, some of them requiring skill in judgment. Since there were so few, it was not worthwhile to train a clerk to deal with them and they were therefore styled by the investigator. Of this total, 117 were straightforwardly clerical; that is, only rearrangement of existing headings or

spacing changes were required. The remaining 101 headings
(those requiring addition of parenthetical expressions or
dates, or of a location designation to a place name) required
some verification. In most cases it was feasible to devise
a parenthetical modification on the basis of the class number, scope note, or cross references appearing with the
heading. The Encyclopaedia Britannica was consulted as an
authority for those dates which had to be supplied. These
may not be the precise ones which exhaustive search might
provide, but they cover the time periods in question adequately for the purpose.

When all these corrections and additions had been
made the headings were computer-sorted by a preliminary
version of a program written by Stuart Scott. This program
removed all the punctuation and symbols from the record,
storing them in a shadow field, and padded all numbers to
the same length by means of zeros to the left. After sorting, it replaced the punctuation and removed the non-signifi-
cant zeros.

Editing After First Sort

The sorted headings were printed out and scanned.
Typographical errors which had not previously been caught
were corrected. Punching errors in 436 headings, or 4.6
percent of the total, were detected and corrected at this
time.

While styling changes were made in 21.2 percent of
the sample, only 10.4 percent (989 headings) of the sample
of styled headings file at all differently from the way they
are filed in the subject heading list. The bulk of these
headings are those where several files (as under Art) are
now merged into one.

In addition, seventy-one errors in styling (0.7 percent of the sample, 3.4 percent of the total number of headings in which changes were made) were detected and corrected. Almost exactly one-third (24) of these corrections resulted from a policy change made part way through the study. Chronological subdivisions using numbered centuries (e.g., 19th century) originally were not changed, but it was later determined that filing would be affected in some cases. These subdivisions were then modified to include the opening and closing years of the century, e.g., 1800-1900. Of the remaining forty-seven styling errors, the omissions were distributed as follows:

Hyphenated compound words
    to be made two words   5
    to be made a single word   4

Parenthetical expressions
    to be added   6
    to be changed to dashed subdivisions   1

Inversions
    changed to dashed subdivision   1
    changed to dashed subdivision and
      trailing preposition deleted   1

Place names requiring addition of
    location designation   3

Dates to be added or shifted   10

Abbreviations to be written out   6

Numerals to be inverted   3

Separable prefix   1

Initialism requiring spaces between
    the letters   1

Initial articles to be deleted (not originally provided for by the rules but included in the computer filing code)   2

The remaing three styling errors involved changes in parenthetical expressions:

From subfield to removal of parentheses
around a prepositional phrase   1

From dashed subdivision to a subfield   2

The relatively simple procedure for styling subject headings was not intended to produce correct and useful results in every case. Rather, the object was to design a procedure that would produce such results nearly all the time, permitting the services of highly skilled professionals, if used at all, to be used only for the exceptional cases. The exceptional cases in this instance were of three main varieties.

1. Inverted prepositional phrases, which upon removal of the trailing preposition and change of the comma to a dash became ambiguous or awkward (25 cases).

2. Other headings which were made ambiguous or awkward by the styling procedure (13 cases).

3. Headings which were originally hyphenated compound words, and in which the heading and see reference to it file next to each other under the procedure as in the example below (22 cases).

LC headings

Hitch-hiking
    See Hitchhiking
Hitches
    See Slings and hitches
Hitchhiking

Styled headings

Hitches
    See Slings and hitches
Hitchhiking
Hitchhiking
    See Hitchhiking

All the ambiguous or awkward headings described above which were found in the first sort are listed in Tables 20 and 21 respectively, together with a suggested form which takes into consideration the sequence of headings in the immediate neighborhood. Most of the awkward headings result from changing inversions to dashed subdivisions.

Of the twenty-five headings which were inverted prepositional phrases in their original LC form and which were made ambiguous or awkward by the styling procedure, nineteen are see references. The usefulness of some of these references may be questioned, but it would be outside the scope of this study to do so. The Library of Congress form was restored for twelve headings (numbered "1" in Table 20) which were unique up to the first punctuation mark, since filing of these headings would not be affected by any changes. In four other cases (numbered "2") the LC form was restored because the inversion was of a proper name and no other form would have been as useful.

The remaining nine headings (numbered "3") were then changed to the heading-subdivision form, but the preposition was kept. Five of these represent true aspects of the subject.

All the headings beginning with the word State are cross-references; the subdivision form produces a consistent file. Finally, the reference Knowledge, Books of is of questionable utility regardless of the form in which it is expressed. It may also be expressed as a dashed subdivision for the sake of consistency.

Most of the thirteen headings in Table 21 were originally inversions and headings which became ambiguous or awkward by their association with them. Six of these

TABLE 20: Headings made ambiguous or awkward by styling procedure: inverted prepositional phrases

	LC heading	Styled heading	Suggested modification
(1)	Bethsaida, Blind Man at (Miracle) See...	Bethsaida - Blind Man (Miracle)	Use LC form
(3)	Cities and towns, Movement to See...	Cities and towns - Movement	Cities and towns - Movement to
(2)	England, Church of See...	England - Church	Use LC form
(3)	Evil, Non-resistance to	Evil - Non-resistance	Evil - Non-resistance to
(1)	Fire damages, Liability for See...	Fire damages - Liability	Use LC form
(1)	Flexible surfaces, Equilibrium of See...	Flexible surfaces - Equilibrium	Use LC form
(1)	Inquiry, Courts of See...	Inquiry - Courts	Use LC form
(3)	Knowledge, Books of See...	Knowledge - Books	Knowledge - Books of (or omit reference entirely)
(2)	Knowledge, Tree of See...	Knowledge - Tree	Use LC form
(3)	Music, Imitation in See...	Music - Imitation	Music - Imitation in
(3)	Music, Impressionism in	Music - Impressionism	Music - Impressionism in

TABLE 20: continued

	LC heading	Styled heading	Suggested modification
(2)	Obedience, Oath of, 1606 See...	Obedience – Oath, 1606	Use LC form
(2)	Obedience, Vow of	Obedience – Vow	Use LC form
(3)	Proof, Burden of See...	Proof – Burden	Proof – Burden of
(1)	Royal descent, Families of	Royal descent – Families	Use LC form
(1)	Sacred Heart, Devotion to	Sacred Heart – Devotion	Use LC form
(1)	Sacred Heart, Feast of the	Sacred Heart – Feast	Use LC form
(1)	Sacred Heart of Jesus, Devotion to See...	Sacred Heart of Jesus – Devotion	Use LC form
(1)	Sacred Heart of Mary, Devotion to See...	Sacred Heart of Mary – Devotion	Use LC form
(1)	Sorrows of Our Lady, Devotion to See...	Sorrows of Our Lady – Devotion	Use LC form
(1)	Sorrows of the Blessed Virgin Mary, Devotion to	Sorrows of the Blessed Virgin Mary – Devotion	Use LC form
(3)	State, Act of See...	State – Act	State – Act of
(3)	State, Heads of See...	State – Heads	State – Heads of
(3)	State, Matter of See...	State – Matter	State – Matter of
(1)	Supper, Parable of See...	Supper – Parable	Use LC form

TABLE 21: Headings made ambiguous or awkward by styling procedure: other forms

	LC heading	Styled heading	Suggested modification
(1)	Currency, Occupation See...	Currency - Occupation	Use LC form
(1)	Immersion, Baptismal See...	Immersion - Baptismal	Use LC form
(1)	Immersion, Heat of See...	Immersion - Heat	Use LC form
(3)	Insurance, War risk	Insurance - War risk	Use scope note in LC list
(3)	Insurance - War risks	Insurance - War risks	Use styled heading
(1)	Judgment, Last See...	Judgment - Last	Use LC form
(1)	Lens, Crystalline See...	Lens - Crystalline	Use LC form
(2)	State, The	State - The	State
(1)	Washers (for bolts and screws)	Washers for bolts and screws	Use LC form
(3)	Worms, Concordat of, 1122 See...	Worms - Concordat, 1122	Worms (City) - Concordat, 1122
(3)	Worms, Diet of, 1521	Worms - Diet, 1521	Worms (City) - Diet, 1521
(3)	Worms, Fossil	Worms - Fossil	Worms (Animals) - Fossil
(3)	Worms, Intestinal and parasitic	Worms - Intestinal and Parasitic	Worms (Animals) - Intestinal and parasitic

(numbered "1" in the table) were restored to their original
LC form because they did not conflict with other headings in
this form. Furthermore, the one parenthetical expression,
while it is a prepositional phrase, is also an explanation of
the meaning of the term as used and should therefore be
kept in parentheses.

The heading, State, The (number "2") would, no
matter how it was phrased, file on The unless the word
were omitted. This is one occasion (and the only one in the
sample) where use of the non-printing symbol to indicate
material to be ignored in filing would have been highly useful.

The headings beginning with the words Insurance and
Worms (number "3") appear in the table because their association with each other creates ambiguity. The scope note
already appearing in the LC list under the heading Insurance,
War risk serves to differentiate it from the heading, Insurance - War risks, so these two headings may be left in
their modified form. Addition of parenthetical expressions
serves to distinguish the city of Worms from the animal.

The changes described immediately above were not
made for the second and final sort. The sort includes only
the headings produced by the standard styling procedure,
with the typographical and styling errors corrected.

In the cases where heading and cross reference were
made to file continuously because hyphenated compound
words were brought into conformity with Webster's dictionary, the see references may be changed into a form that will
file as one word if the heading files as two or vice-versa.
The same applies to some cross references from subdivisions
to the inverted form. Table 22 lists these headings: (1) in

TABLE 22: Headings and cross-references which would file together by styling procedure

LC form	Styled form	Suggested modification of See Reference
Bot-flies See Botflies	Botflies	Bot flies
Bower-birds See Bowerbirds	Bower-birds Bowerbirds	Bower birds
Clearing-house See Clearinghouse	Clearinghouse	Clearing house
Drop-outs See Dropouts	Dropouts	Drop outs
Fire-boats See Fireboats	Fireboats	Fire boats
God - Fear See Fear of God God, Fear of See Fear of God	God - Fear	Only 1 ref. req.
Hitch-hiking See Hitchhiking	Hitchhiking	Hitch hiking
Journalism - Agriculture See Journalism, Agricultural	Journalism - Agriculture Journalism - Agricultural	Omit
Journalism - Commerce See Journalism, Commercial	Journalism - Commerce Journalism - Commerical	Omit

TABLE 22 : continued

LC form	Styled form	Suggested modification of See Reference
Journalism - Labor See Journalism, Labor	Journalism - Labor	Omit
Journalism - Medicine See Journalism, Medical	Journalism - Medicine Journalism - Medical	Omit
Journalism, Negro See Negro press Journalism - Negroes See Negro press	Journalism - Negro	Omit
Journalism - Religion See Journalism, Religious	Journalism - Religion Journalism - Religious	Omit
Juchen (Tribe) See Ju-chen (Tribe)	Juchen (Tribe) Ju-Chen (Tribe)	Ju Chen (Tribe)
Music, Physiological effect of See Music - Physiological effect	Music - Physiological effect	Omit
Paper-weights See Paperweights	Paperweights	Paper weights
Rubber - Reclaiming See Rubber, Reclaimed	Rubber - Reclaiming Rubber - Reclaimed	Omit
Teachers, Certification of See Teachers - Certification	Teachers - Certification	Omit

TABLE 22: continued

LC form	Styled form	Suggested modification of See Reference
Treaties, Revision of See Treaties - Revision	Treaties - Revision	Omit
Tuberculosis, Mortality from See Tuberculosis - Mortality	Tuberculosis - Mortality	Omit
Tzel-tal Indians See Tzeltal Indians	Tzel-tal Indians Tzeltal Indians	Tzel tal Indians
Tzel-tal language See Tzeltal language	Tzel-tal language Tzeltal language	Tzel tal language

their original LC form; (2) as styled by the procedure; and
(3) as modified so that the see reference may perform its
function. Other intervening headings are not shown.

After all the errors, both typographic and styling,
were corrected on the punched cards, the cards were sorted
again by the same program described above. One addition
was made to the program when it was discovered that some
headings used B. C. dates as filing elements. This new
program segment senses the B of B. C. in the character
position immediately following the number, and arranges
B. C. dates in reverse order (larger before smaller numbers)
and before all A. D. dates. This feature adds to the time
required for pre- and post-sort formatting; since there were
only eight B. C. dates in the sample, the only reason for
adding it to the program was to demonstrate its feasibility.

Summary

Many of the limitations of this study have been evident, but they should be summarized here. Only the form
of subject headings, not the content, was considered. For
practical purposes, this meant taking as given the heading
up to the first punctuation mark. Except for the hyphen,
punctuation marks usually denote subordination or relation
of some kind, and punctuation has--with considerable varia-
tion--been used as a filing element in the past. Therefore,
the punctuation mark was the logical place to begin the
regularization process. The set of rules devised uses
punctuation marks in two ways: as they are conventionally
used in English grammar, and as part of a special grammar
of subject headings. The comma in series is an example of
the former, and the dashed subdivision is an example of the

latter. No changes were made in the first sort of use; as the second is highly specialized to this one area, it is legitimate to change it in that area.

Some of the subject headings produced are certainly open to question. In particular, the opening and closing dates of major historical periods are difficult to assign precisely. One is, however, inevitably led to suspect that assignment of actual book titles to these historical periods is likely to be just as difficult. Opening and closing dates must be regarded as implicit in the heading. Further research on the time scope of individual headings might permit more careful date assignment. It would not affect the feasibility of the method, which has been adequately demonstrated.

The same reservation could apply to those hyphenated compound words which were not altered because they did not appear in Webster II. More specialized works could provide authority for them all, but such a procedure would be in the nature of authority work, and outside the scope of this study.

The subsidiary purpose of the study was to devise a styling procedure that was as simple as possible, preferably clerical in level. This aim was partially achieved. The only major problem arose with regard to parenthetical expressions--evidence of the varying purposes for which this form has been used. The refinements made after the headings were styled would improve application, but considerable professional attention would still be necessary. It would be simple to select on the computer all the headings containing parenthetical expressions and print them out for inspection, together with the headings surrounding them.

One measure of the usefulness of the procedure is

that only thirty-seven headings (less than 0.4 percent of the total sample, or 1.8 percent of the headings in which styling changes were made) were made ambiguous or awkward.

Another measure, not of usefulness but of just how radical are the changes involved, is the number of headings whose filing position is changed. This proportion is significant, some 10.4 percent of the total sample, but a great many of these headings are part of large groups, all of which were moved, e.g., the headings beginning Insurance or Art. When headings of which only one or two begin with the same characters up to the first punctuation mark (excluding the hyphen) are considered, only 238, or about 2.4 percent of the entire sample, are changed in position. The other headings which file differently are primarily those which were part of long files of several sub-alphabets, especially the inversions which were changed to dashed subdivisions and the different kinds of dashed subdivisions. This interfiling is in accord with the new ALA filing rules, but not with most other rules.

The important question, one for which further investigation with an entirely different emphasis from that of this study would be required, is the desirability of such sub-arrangements. It is almost certain, however, that without definite, clear cues to the filer and user that the sub-arrangements are present, they are not very useful. The punctuation used today does not offer such cues. It is highly likely that the sub-arrangements used represent an ad hoc faceting system, and that some means might be devised to represent this system unambiguously by means of alphabetic or numeric characters.

With the reservation described above, the study has

demonstrated that subject headings can be so styled as to
file unambiguously on the computer.

Notes

1. This study was supported in part by U.S. Office of
    Education Grant Number OEC-1-7-178045-3545.

2. William R. Nugent, "The Mechanization of the Filing
    Rules for the Dictionary Catalogs of the Library of
    Congress," Library Resources and Technical
    Services, XI (Spring, 1967), 145-166.

3. Interviews with John Rather, July 23-25, 1968.

4. Theodore C. Hines and Jessica L. Harris, Computer
    Filing of Index, Bibliographic and Catalog Entries.

5. Ibid.

6. It should be noted that this means the sort routine
    makes no limitation on input or printout. The print
    chain may have any refinements desired, including
    capital and lower-case letters.

7. American Library Association, ALA Rules for Filing
    Catalog Cards, 1st ed.

8. American Library Association, Rules, 2nd ed.

9. Ibid., p. 1.

10. U.S. Library of Congress, Filing Rules for the Dic-
    tionary Catalogs of the Library of Congress.

11. Daily, "The Grammar of Subject Headings."

12. Ibid., p. 87-89.

13. Ibid., p. 117.

14. Ibid., p. 119-120.

Chapter VII

Cross Reference Policy

No matter how good the system used for structuring subject headings, many of the concepts cannot be expressed by a single word; and while in some instances it is immediately clear what the entry word in a multiple-word heading should be, this is not usually the case. It might be possible to devise a system of structuring subject headings such that the entry word was always predictable to one who knew the system, but such systems seem always to be inflexible. The work of Prévost is an example.[1]

Any system, such as the one used by the Library of Congress, which does not require the form of expression of every subject to fit a set of inflexible rules, must provide a cross reference structure to guide users from those forms of expression of a subject not chosen as entry points to the one which is. Any system, even an inflexible one, would require cross referencing from unused synonyms. The type of cross references under consideration here are those which lead from different forms of expression of a subject to the one actually used.

The making of cross references is unavoidably dependent to a certain extent on the skill and memory of the cataloger responsible; however, for some kinds of headings it is likely that in all or nearly all cases a cross reference from a different form of heading might be useful. For example, perhaps all inverted headings should be referred to

199

from the direct form; all terms which are used as subdivisions under place names might receive a general cross reference (see or see also) from the term used as subject; when terms are connected by "and," a reference from the term following the connective might be advisable. Examples of kinds of headings to which a general policy would surely not be applicable are all subject subdivisions, and adjectival phrases entered directly. (The latter is the reverse of inversion, but in many cases, e.g., Acyloin reaction, the non-entry word is a general term, so that a policy of always cross referencing from the second word would not be practicable.)

The purpose of this study was to determine the extent to which a general policy of making (or not making) see or see also references had been followed for kinds of headings to which such a policy would be applicable. While there might be many kinds of headings for which such a policy might be made, only certain major types were selected for study. Unless otherwise stated, the sample in each case consisted of all the used main headings (i.e., not cross references) of the appropriate type that were found in the 10 percent sample used for most of the rest of the study, with the following limitations. It became clear during the analysis that certain modifications of terms were treated (for purposes of cross referencing at least) exactly as though they were subject subdivisions, i.e., the subject heading without the modification would receive cross references of the type under consideration, but the term with modification did not receive such cross references. Such a policy would make sense, because these modifications all file together, and they are true subdivisions of the main heading, just like

subdivisions using the dash.   For this reason such modifications were omitted from the analysis.   The particular
kinds of modifications (other than dashed subdivisions) which
were ignored are described below and examples given, together with the description of the types of headings for which
cross reference policy was studied.

    1. Inversions. --The direct forms of these headings
were checked to see if reference had been made.   Haykin[2]
specifies a reference from the direct form of inverted adjectival headings.   If the inverted part of the heading consisted of more than one entity joined by and and/or of a
series (e.g., Tuberculosis, Congenital, hereditary, and in-
fantile), each member of the phrase was checked.   When an
inversion occurred both with and without parenthetical expressions (e.g., Evidence, Criminal; Evidence, Criminal
(Frankish law)), the heading(s) with the expressions were
omitted.   Music headings of the form, Trumpet and drum
music, Arranged, were included, while (where a heading of
the form just mentioned occurred) headings of the form,
Trumpet and drum with band, Arranged, were excluded.   The
latter form is clearly a sort of subdivision of the former.
Inversions within parenthetical expressions (e.g., (Canon law,
Orthodox Eastern)), were also excluded.

    2. Terms used as subdivisions under places. --The
requirement here would be for a general see also or see
reference, depending on whether it was used as an independent subject heading or not, from the term standing alone.
Haykin calls for a general reference from such terms.[3]
There were not enough terms of the type required in the
sample; therefore, subdivisions of certain major countries,
states and cities in the list were checked whether they

occurred in the sample or not. The exclusions here were of
three types: (1) some subdivisions were used both without
and with an inverted adjective (e.g., U.S. - Statistics; U.S.
- Statistics, Vital), and the latter were excluded in these
cases; (2) subdivisions such as Relations (general) with
[country] and Claims vs. [country] were counted only once
for a given main heading, no matter how many times they
appeared; (3) such subdivisions as Siege, [date] were counted
only once for a given place, even if more than one siege was
listed. A listing of the places used is included in the discussion of this investigation.

　　　　3.　Parenthetical expressions. --Due to the nature of
many of these expressions a general see or see also reference is to be anticipated if any reference at all is made.
No parenthetical expressions in used main headings were
excluded.

　　　　4.　Compound headings such as "Good and evil."--
Search was made for references from the word following and.
Haykin calls for a reference from the heading with the names
transposed, or from the word following and. [4] Exclusions
include all the exclusions listed under Inversions (1), plus
those inversions in which an and phrase occurs as the
second part of the heading.

Inversions

　　　　There were 515 inverted headings in the sample. Of
these, nine were of the form Worms, Intestinal and para-
sitic, where the adjective is replaced by a pair of adjectives
connected by and or by a two- or three-member series.
These headings were each treated as two or three headings
for purposes of checking the references, making a total of

526 headings. It was necessary to break these headings down because their treatment in the list ran the full gamut from none of the parts being referenced, through references from one or both parts, to reference from the full uninverted heading.

Table 23 summarizes the findings of the study. The typical practice has been to make a reference of some sort from the direct form of a heading when the inverted form has been chosen for entry. Over half the inverted headings in the sample are specifically referred to from the direct form. In another 31 percent of cases, there was an adequate substitute: a general cross reference, or a reference from a slightly different form.

The few headings to which see or see also references were made from other than the direct form or a close equivalent present some difficulty. There are not enough of them for a pattern to be established with any certainty; however, it would appear that in most cases the existing form was selected because it would thus be possible to fit a reference beginning with the desired word into the existing pattern of headings.

As for the headings for which there were no references, there is no real distinguishing factor to show why they were treated thus. In many cases the adjective is one designating language or nationality, but many such headings are referred to from the direct form. In twenty-four headings of the type, Piano and organ music, Arranged, the apparent inversion is clearly a cataloger's device, and a long list of references such as Arranged piano and organ music would be of little use. For this reason these headings were omitted from the calculations.

TABLE 23:   See and see also references from direct to
inverted heading forms

	Number	Percent
See reference present	271	54
No specific reference, but adequate substitute found	153	31
General reference applicable 143		
Conjunctive adjectives from which referencing adequate 9		
References from noun form of word subdivided 1		
Subtotal	424	85
Other types of reference	17	3
See also from the word alone, or from another phrase beginning with the word 10		
See from another phrase beginning with the word 7		
Subtotal	441	88
No cross referencing	61	12
Total	502	100

No reference to be anticipated, as
heading is not a true inversion
(use of direct form in text
would be unlikely)   24

It is clear that the Library of Congress usually makes some sort of reference from the direct to the inverted form of subject headings, but this is not a consistently followed policy.

Subdivisions of Geographical Names

There was one possible problem in this analysis: most geographic names are also used as corporate names. However, it became clear that this distinction did not have any particular effect on treatment of subdivisions, so no attempt was made to separate the two uses. Furthermore, in most cases where a place name is used as a corporate name, the name of some organization in the hierarchy appears as part of the heading, thereby eliminating a large portion of such entries automatically.

Table 24 presents a tabulation of the references found for these subdivisions. These represent all dashed subdivisions in the LC subject heading list for the following places:

Africa
America
Boston
Chicago
France
Italy
New York   (City)
New York   (State)
U. S.

Since many of the subdivisions were used under more than one heading, they were tabulated in two ways: (1) counting each one once only, the first time it appeared; and (2) counting each one each time it appeared. The table shows that the differences in the pattern are small.

Several different forms of reference are distinguished in the table. The first is that of a general see or see also

TABLE 24:   Cross references to terms used as subdivisions
under place names

	Unique subdivisions		Total subdivisions	
	No.	%	No.	%
General see or see also reference from term as main heading	79	66	157	75
General see also reference from plural of term	8	7	11	5
General or specific reference from other form of term	19	16	24	12
Subtotal	106	89	192	92
No reference	13	11	17	8
Total	119	100	209	100

reference from the term (in exactly the same form as it was
used as a subdivision) as a main heading.   The second group
includes all terms which as subdivisions were used in the
singular, but the plural form was used as a main heading.
This group includes headings such as Sieges and Blizzards,
from which see also references are made to specific sieges
and blizzards as subdivisions under place names.   Finally,
there are the references from the term in a different form,
but beginning with some form of the same word as the subdivision began with.   There is not much point in distinguishing among these categories; the category is almost certainly
determined by the form chosen for the main heading versus
the form chosen for the subdivision.   If both headings and
subdivisions are taken as given, the references in each case

are those to be expected.

A general policy has been followed for making references from the term used as main heading to the same term used as a subdivision under place names. This policy has been followed in approximately 90 percent of cases. The reason for non-observance of this policy in the remaining 10 percent is not clear. The subdivisions to which reference was not made are listed below. For a few of the subdivisions, such as the first one, it is clear that no form of reference would be useful, but others could quite legitimately be referred from. Boston - Garrison mob, 1835, is an example.

America - Early accounts to 1600
America - Politics
Boston - Garrison mob, 1835
New York (City) - Description
New York (City) - Garment Workers' Strike,
                            1912-1913
U.S. - Colonial question
U.S. - Description and travel
U.S. - Exploring expeditions
U.S. - Insular possessions
U.S. - Relations (general) with foreign countries
U.S. - Social life and customs
U.S. - Territorial expansion
U.S. - Territories and possessions

Parenthetical Expressions

Daily searched for cross references from a sample of the terms in parentheses in the fifth edition of the LC subject heading list.[5] His sample was drawn from those terms which appeared only once as parenthetical expressions. In addition, he checked some of the terms which appeared most often as parenthetical expressions. In the sample of 179 of 302 unique expressions, he found 90 with no reference

from the term, and 89 with some sort of see or see also
reference. However, he gives no indication of any further
analysis of these terms. In his checking of terms which
appeared very often in parentheses, he does not accept general see also references of the form found under <u>Canon law</u>
"<u>sa</u>... Church discipline (Canon law); Dioceses (Canon law)
and similar headings," as functioning as references to <u>all</u>
headings followed by <u>Canon law</u> in parentheses.

The purpose of the study reported here was to determine if evidence could be found of any general policy of
cross referencing from terms in parentheses to the same
terms used as main headings. In accordance with this purpose all parenthetical terms in the sample were checked.
No distinctions between unique and non-unique terms were
made; terms in series, numbers and function words were
not excluded. (These were the limitations imposed by Daily.)

The form of cross reference to be anticipated from
terms in parenthetical expressions may be expected to vary.
In fact, there are some types from which no cross reference
would be useful. The parenthetical term may be of a type
which would be useless as a main heading, such as <u>Aviation
mechanics (Persons)</u>. In other cases a phrase explaining the
heading might conceivably be used (in some form) as a heading itself, but the phrase is purely explanatory, and does not
indicate a category to which the term belongs; <u>Snake devices
(American colonies)</u> is an example.

Some parenthetical expressions, primarily those found
in music headings, are exactly analogous to subdivisions,
and no use would be served by a reference. An example is
<u>Trumpets (2) with orchestra.</u> There were only fifteen head-
ings, out of 321 in the sample, to which no reference from

the term in parenthese would have been useful.

From all the other terms used in parenthetical expressions, some form of cross reference could be useful. The form would vary depending on the heading. If the parenthetical term does not appear in the list as a main heading, then a see reference would be used. If the term does appear as a main heading, but in a different form-- such as direct in the parenthetical expression, but inverted as an independent heading--then a general or specific see also reference might be made from the term in its main heading form.

Table 25 shows the kinds of references made from terms used as parenthetical expressions. Over one-third of these expressions specified a system of law, such as Adat law; Canon law, Orthodox Eastern; or Maya law. All these systems of law are used as subject headings, some in the direct and some in the inverted form. Furthermore, in all cases there is a see also reference from the name of the system of law, either generally to "specific legal headings with [the system] added in parentheses...,"[6] or specifically to the actual headings. It is clear that for these legal headings a policy of cross referencing has been adopted and carried out. The single variant heading is Support (Domestic relations law, Hindu), which has a cross reference from Hindu law. The reason for this variant is, it may be supposed, the heading immediately preceding: Support (Domestic relations), the cross references to and from which indicate that the legal sense of the term is included in its scope.

Policy for non-legal headings is not nearly so clear. If a reference is made at all, the type (see or see also from the same or a similar form, or see also from a

TABLE 25:   Cross references from terms in parentheses

Description	Number headings	% of total	% of total non-legal headings
Legal headings with general or specific see also	108	35	
Legal heading with variant reference	1		
Non-legal headings with practically identical see or see also	79	26	40
Non-legal headings with comparable see also	51	17	26
See reference or duplicate entry from parenthetical expression as main heading, and access term as sub-division	3	1	2
Subtotal	242	79	68
No useful reference	64	21	32
Total	306	100	100
No reference from term in parentheses would be useful	15		

comparable form), is determined by the form used in the
list for the concept represented by the term in parentheses.
Almost one-third of the non-legal headings containing parenthetical expressions were not referred to from any variant
of the term in parentheses.   The criteria for determining if
an acceptable reference existed were purposely made as loose

as possible, although a distinction was made between references from essentially identical forms (the only differences
being such ones as those between singular and plural, or
between direct and inverted entry), and references from
comparable terms.   Examples of the latter are:

> Royal supremacy (Church of England)
>   xx Church of England - Government
> MAD (Computer program language)
>   xx Programming languages (Electronic com-
> Boston (Dance)   puters)
>   xx Dancing

Most of these comparable references are in a form which is
determined by the manner in which the concept is expressed
as a heading.

In these categories there were only a few see references, so no distinction was made between see and see also
references.

The last "useful" group of references is small (only
three items) but distinct from the others.   Both duplicate
entry and see references occur here.   These are cases in
which some variant of the parenthetical expression was used
as a main heading, and the original access term became a
subdivision.   Examples are:

> Flaps (Aeroplanes)
>   x Aeroplanes - Flaps
> Finnish poetry (Swedish) with duplicate entry:
> Swedish poetry - Finnish authors

A few headings were omitted from the sample because
no useful cross reference from any variant of the term in
parentheses would have been of value.   Examples are:

> Aviation mechanics (Persons)
> Inscriptions, Turkish (Old)
> Scaticook Indians (Conn.)
> Trumpets (2) with orchestra
> Names of cities and provinces followed by (City)
>   or (Province), respectively

No clear reason for the failure to assign cross references to non-legal headings is evident. The proportion of headings without cross referencing is high enough to warrant a conclusion that if there has been a policy of making cross references from terms in parentheses, it has not been consistently followed for non-legal headings.

Headings Containing "and"

There were a total of 129 headings in the sample which satisfied the criteria for this category. In the analysis several conditions proved to have some effect on the likelihood of reference being made from the word following and, i.e., the word which was not the access point. Among these conditions were:

1. Whether nouns or adjectives were connected by the conjunction.
2. Whether the phrase was simple or complex; i.e., of the form [noun 1] and [noun 2] or of some such form as [adjective noun 1] and [noun 2].
3. Whether, if the reference were made, it would fall next to the heading itself in the subject heading list.

If an adjective applied to both of a pair of nouns connected by and, search was made not under the second noun but under the adjective, followed by the second noun. Table 26 shows a tabulation of the categories above. Nine headings could not be fitted into these categories. Three of these were referred to from a heading beginning with some form of the word following and, but the heading was of a different structure. These were:

Cleaning and dyeing industry
xx Dyes and dyeing

TABLE 26: Headings containing "and"

	Reference No.	%	No reference No.	%
I. Nouns connected by "and"				
A. Simple headings				
1. Reference would be next heading	2	2	7	6
2. Other headings would intervene	52	43	5	4
B. Complex headings				
1. Reference would be next heading	2	2	6	5
2. Other headings would intervene	8	7	19	16
Subtotal	64	54	37	31
II. Adjectives connected by "and"				
A. Simple headings				
Other headings would intervene	18	15		
B. Complex headings				
Reference would be next heading			1	1
Total	82	69	38	32
Totals:				
Simple headings	72	60	12	10
Complex headings	10	8	26	22
Reference would be next heading	4	3	14	12
Other headings would intervene	78	65	24	20

Art and mythology
   x Mythology in art
Plant cells and tissues
   x Tissues, Vegetable

The remaining six headings are all for ballads and songs,
preceded by a specification of language, e.g., English ballads and songs. The reference to be searched for in this
case is English songs; however, the heading Songs, English
is used for collections including music while English ballads
and songs is used for collections including words only.
Therefore, the reference from English songs is to Songs,
English, but there is a see also reference to the latter
heading from English ballads and songs.

Table 26 shows that the see reference policy described by Haykin for headings using "and" is not always followed. However, in several of the categories a clear-cut
preference is evident. Group IA2, of which only five headings were not referred to, contains nearly half of the headings in the sample. Simple headings were much more likely
to be referred to than complex ones; perhaps partly because
the latter would begin with the same word. Among the
relatively small number of cases where the reference would
fall next to the used heading in the list cross references
are usually not made. Probably they should not be made at
all, since these headings are virtually all of the type represented by Snobs and snobbishness. The total is too small
to permit certain conclusions, but it would appear that when
adjectives are connected by "and," the reference is always
made, except when it would be the next heading. However,
comparison with the equivalent subcategories in the noun
category shows that this result is probably due to the small
size of the sample: simple headings are very likely to be

referred to if the reference would not be adjacent to the
heading, regardless of whether they fall into the noun or the
adjective category.

Summary

The four types of headings investigated are, if not
actually the most important, among the most important types
of headings for which a general policy of making cross
references from a part of the heading which is not the access point would be conceivable and useful. A clear policy
of cross referencing is evident for three of the four types of
headings, if the variant forms of references are accepted as
valid. It is necessary to do this if the forms and structure
of headings are taken as given, as they are for the purposes
of this study.

At the 95 percent confidence level, 79 ± 5 percent of
parenthetical expressions, 92 ± 4 percent of subdivisions of
place names, and 88 ± 3 percent of inversions are referred
from. These proportions are high, but there is room for
serious questioning as to why they are not higher. Furthermore, if only non-legal parenthetical expressions are considered, the proportion of references drops to 68 ± 6 percent.
Terms following and are only referred from 69 ± 8 percent
of the time, showing a tendency to make, but not a policy
of making, such references.

The policies suggested here are not intended to be
absolute, but would simply consist of a statement that such
references would be made unless there were a reason not to
do so. It is surely preferable to have a few unneeded references in the catalog than to omit significant numbers of useful ones. Such policies--which could be extended to cate-

gories of headings other than those discussed here--could
cut down on the decisions required of the cataloger by making an important group of references more or less automatically.

Notes

1. Prévost, "Approach to Theory and Method."

2. Haykin, Subject Headings, p. 22.

3. Ibid., p. 20.

4. Ibid., p. 24.

5. Daily, "The Grammar of Subject Headings," p. 88-95.

6. Cf. the reference under Adat law in the LC subject
   heading list.

Chapter VIII

Summary and Conclusions

Background of the study

The need for a comprehensive code for subject heading work has long been recognized, but there has been so little research in the area of form and structure of subject headings and the subject catalog that even the first requirement of a code--definition of present practice--could not be met, except in a very few areas. The state of the art has not really advanced a great deal since the publication of the first edition of Cutter's Rules in 1876. Even much of what is generally thought to be true of subject headings is not backed up by actual evidence. It has always been known that the subject catalog was not fulfilling its functions as well as it should--whatever these functions were considered to be. The situation has become even more acute in recent years, with the simultaneous increase in publication and in library book budgets. A system that works even fairly well in a library of a given size may break down completely when the collection increases in size by an order of magnitude within a few years--and this kind of increase has not been unknown in recent years.

A further complicating factor is use of the computer and other mechanical devices to perform tasks which were originally built around the abilities of human beings. Many characteristics of the subject catalog are present simply be-

218   Subject Analysis

cause the system grew without much advance planning, and
humans could deal with the results.   To use a computer
effectively requires at least a minimum of systematization.
To use people as effectively as possible also requires systematization.
    This study was undertaken to provide descriptions of
present subject heading practice in certain important areas,
based on a belief that it is not useful to propose new practices without determining the value of the old.
          Certain assumptions were basic to the study.   These
were that:

    1. Subject access to materials provides a use-
       ful form of bibliographic control.

    2. Some form of access similar to the alpha-
       betico-specific subject heading will continue
       to be useful and used.

    3. Once the entry term has been selected, the
       grammatical structure adopted for the terms
       of a heading is largely determined by the
       need to find the best possible location in the
       existing structure for the new heading.

    4. Usage of terms in the English language is a
       major factor in selection of the terms of a
       subject heading.

    Six hypotheses bearing on important factors in the
form and structure of subject headings and the subject catalog were formulated.   These were that:

    1. Two major factors in introduction of aspect
       subdivisions of specific subjects are:

       a) Avoidance of long files under a given
       heading.

       b) The need to bring out the existence of a
       significant number of books on a given as-
       pect of the subject, even when the size of

the total file under the subject is not particularly large.

2. Use of inverted adjective-noun combinations, in preference to:

   a) Direct entry of these combinations, is dependent on which of the two words may be regarded as best specifying the subject.

   b) Subdivision by means of the dash, is used to achieve a classified subarrangement by use of punctuation marks (for example, <u>Cookery, American</u> could be written as <u>Cookery - America,</u> if it were preferred to arrange it in the same file as <u>Cookery - History</u>).

3. Choice of the subject heading proper (exclusive of aspect subdivision) for application to the same books is not dependent on the nature, size, or objectives of the general library collections for which subject cataloging is designed.

4. Application of form headings and headings denoting the type (e.g., <u>Fiction</u> as a heading for novels), rather than the subject, of a work, is significantly correlated with the size of the file that has accumulated or would accumulate under the heading (i.e., in open stack libraries form headings are used only when there are or would be a small number of entries under the form).

5. Styling of subject headings can be effected in such a way as to make feasible a consistent and meaningful computer arrangement, using (for arrangement) only the characters appearing in the entry.

6. In cases permitting the adoption of a uniform policy for establishment of cross references (for example, from the direct to the inverted form of heading when the latter has been used), no consistent policy has been followed in the LC list.

The study was in general limited to subject headings
intended for collections whose subject scope was general,
and to monographic materials.   If these limitations had not
been imposed, more variables would have been introduced,
and as it was, it was known that only some of several variables influencing each of the areas involved were being
studied.

While subject heading practice in the United States is
quite varied, the influence of the Library of Congress
through its catalog cards and subject heading list is generally acknowledged to provide the basis for most subject
heading work today.   For this reason, LC subject headings
in its list and its official catalog were selected as the universe of study, with Wilson cataloging used when practice in
different types of libraries was being compared.

Methodology

Most of the study was based on analyses of a 10 percent sample of the seventh edition of the LC subject heading
list.   The heading, subdivisions and see references were
keypunched as they appeared in the list and expanded by
computer program to the full form of the heading.   Another
program then produced listings of inversions, words in
series, subdivisions of all levels, parenthetical expressions,
prepositional phrases, connectives, see references, and instructions for direct and indirect geographical subdivision.
All these listings were produced without coding, simply on
the basis of the characteristics of the headings themselves.
Another program produced a listing of all the words appearing in the sample.   Coding was used for the study of styling
for computer arrangement; the codes were punched as part
of the headings, and a computer program made most of the

required changes automatically, printing out a listing by type
of those changes which required human intervention.

Aspect subdivision

A positive correlation of .675 (the true correlation, at
the 95 percent confidence level, is between .631 and .711)
was found between the number of aspect subdivisions of
headings and the number of titles entered under the headings
and their subdivisions (excluding entries under form and
geographic subdivisions). This finding was based on a 5
percent random sample of the used main headings on the
LC subject heading list. The entries and subdivisions of all
the headings in a subsample (0.8 percent) of this sample
were counted in the LC official catalog. When it became
evident that the vast majority of headings had either no aspect subdivisions or only a few, the sample was enlarged to
the 5 percent finally used, and only those headings which
were subdivided in the LC list were counted in the official
catalog.

In its original form, no evidence was found either to
support or to nullify the second part of the hypothesis, but
when it was modified to state that certain subdivisions were
applied to bring out the existence of titles in the area, regardless of the total number of titles entered under the subject, support was found. Form subdivisions are used whenever appropriate; once a decision has been made to subdivide
a heading geographically, such subdivisions are used whenever applicable. Certain subdivisions which are such only
in form are applied whenever they are needed. A major
category of these is events which are entered under the
name of the place where they occurred, subdivided by the
kind of event, e.g., Aachen - Siege, 1944.

Adjective-noun phrases

Assuming that word frequency in natural language
may be regarded as a criterion of degree of specification,
the choice between inversion and direct entry of adjectival
phrases in which the adjective does not refer to an ethnic,
national, linguistic, geographic, or cultural group is influenced by which word best specifies the subject. When the
frequency of the noun is much greater than that of the adjective, the phrase will usually be entered directly, i. e.,
adjective first. Less common nouns are much more likely
to be used as entry words than more common ones. There
is no significant difference between the frequencies of the
nouns and the adjectives in inverted phrases, or between
those of the adjectives in inverted and in direct phrases. It
therefore appears that there may be a tendency to bring the
noun forward by inverting adjectival phrases unless the noun
is of much greater frequency than the adjective.

Word frequency is clearly a major influence in determining whether adjective-noun phrases in which the adjective denotes a national, linguistic, ethnic, cultural or
geographic distinction are entered directly or inverted. The
difference between mean frequency of entry and non-entry
words is significant for all these headings, both direct and
inverted.

Word frequency is associated to a greater or lesser
degree with selection of the entry term in all adjectival
phrases. It is certainly not the only influence, and it is
quite possible that some other factor which happens to be
associated with word frequency is the determining one.
Nevertheless, in structuring new subject headings the relative frequencies of the words involved ought to be a valuable

indicator of the degree of specification afforded by each
alternative.

The hypothesis that inversions and subdivisions of
headings are used to produce a classified sub-arrangement
was verified in large part. Of the ninety-three headings in the
sample which were modified by both inversion and subdivision, 80 percent used the latter for aspect and/or form, and
the former for kinds of subclasses of the subject. In the
remaining 20 percent a classed sub-arrangement with minor
exceptions (usually see references), or a sub-arrangement
using different or additional classes, was present.

Relative scope of headings intended for different types of
collections

In order to determine if there is a significant difference in the scope of the headings applied to the same book
by cataloging services intended for large and for small libraries, the subject headings applied by LC and by the Wilson Company to a sample of recent (1960 and later) titles
cataloged by both services were compared. There was no
difference in the broadness of the headings themselves, but
the Library of Congress is more likely to subdivide, or to
subdivide more minutely.

The H. W. Wilson cataloging service (and that of
Alanar, which was also compared on a smaller scale) applies
large numbers of form or class headings to fiction. While
some of these would probably be useful even in larger libraries, their application does not appear to be the result of
an established coordinated policy. Many of the headings, if
consistently applied, would produce large undifferentiated
files even in many smaller libraries, and/or would duplicate
shelving categories. Subject headings subdivided Fiction are

often applied to books which are not about the subject; for instance, the name of a country so subdivided is likely to be applied to a book which is simply set in the country.

These headings, and similar class headings applied to nonfiction, may be the result of an attempt to provide access to material in relation to subjects included in school curricula. This could be a valuable form of access, but (1) a consistent policy should be devised and publicized; and/or (2) the possibility of other forms of access ought to be investigated. At the very least, it would be helpful to distinguish these headings from true subject headings on the catalog card.

Use of form headings

All the used main headings in the 10 percent sample of the LC list which could conceivably be used to indicate the form rather than the subject of a publication were searched in the LC official catalog. The original intention was to count the number of cards in the appropriate class(es) in the shelflist for each form, and then to determine from the official catalog if the heading was actually applied as a form heading or not. So few of the headings had a one-to-one correspondence with the classification that it was necessary to abandon this procedure. Instead, the headings were searched in the official catalog, and conclusions drawn on the basis of an analysis into broad LC classes.

Except for the very broadest ones, most headings that could be applied to forms of material are so applied. Headings for literary forms are applied only to collections by more than one author, and where the amount of material is large, the parenthetical expressions (Collections) and (Selections: extracts, etc.) are usually applied. Headings

for musical forms and for instrumental groupings required
for particular works are used for collections and individual
works. These headings, incidentally, form a kind of alternate arrangement to the groupings in the LC classification scheme. Other music form headings are generally
applied only to collections in the form.

The few science and technology headings in the
sample are used for the form, with the exception of two
very broad ones. Headings for newspapers and periodicals
(the only form-of-publication headings in the sample) and for
laws and legislation are not used as form headings.

Styling for computer arrangement

It is not feasible to computer-arrange subject headings in their conventional form and their conventional order.
This part of the study was undertaken in order to determine
what sort of arrangement would be possible if a fairly
simple set of styling rules, dealing primarily with punctuation, and using the filing code of Hines and Harris as a
basis for the sort procedure, were devised and applied.

A styling procedure was devised and tested to see if
it could be applied clerically, if it were assumed that the
results of a preliminary sort would be edited to correct
errors and remove ambiguities. Of the 10 percent sample
of the LC list, containing 9,581 headings, 2,071, or 21 percent, required changes. The clerical test of the procedure
was in general successful, though modifications were required in the instructions. The exception was parenthetical
expressions, which in most cases seem to require professional judgment. This may be attributed largely to the fact
that parenthetical expressions have been used for almost
every conceivable purpose.

The headings in which styling changes were to be
made were assigned code numbers, and these were keyed as
part of the heading. A computer program made all the
changes which could be defined simply and unambiguously--
75 percent of the total--and printed out the remainder with
an indication of the change required.

In editing after a preliminary sort, errors were corrected and the few headings made ambiguous or awkward by
the styling procedure were improved in form. There were
only thirty-seven of the latter, an acceptable proportion,
since the procedure was designed to take care of the bulk of
the headings as economically as possible, leaving for professional intervention only those for which it was really
required.

The filing position of 10.4 percent of the headings
was changed by the styling and computer sort, but the vast
majority of these were headings which were part of long files
all beginning with the same word, in which multiple sub-
arrangements formerly present were interfiled. Further
study to determine the desirability of the sub-arrangements
thus eliminated would be valuable, but the basis of any sub-
arrangement used should certainly be made explicit, not left
implicit as at present.

Cross reference policy

Four types of headings were investigated to determine
if a general policy of cross referencing from a part of the
heading other than the entry term had been followed in the
LC list. These types were: parenthetical expressions, inversions, subdivisions of place names, and terms following
and. These are among the most important types of headings
for which such a general policy of cross referencing might
be followed.

The major criterion used was the existence of any
kind of reference, general or specific, see or see also,
from the term under consideration as an entry point, to the
form of entry actually used. Variant forms were accepted
where this was a matter of fitting the reference into the
pattern of entries in the list.

A clear policy of cross referencing is evident for
three of the four types of headings considered. At the 95
percent confidence level, 79 ±5 percent of parenthetical expressions, 92 ±4 percent of subdivisions of place names,
and 88 ±3 percent of inversions are referred from. These
proportions are high, but there is room for considerable
question as to why they are not higher. Furthermore, if
only parenthetical expressions not containing the name of a
system of law are considered, the proportion drops to
68 ±6 percent. Terms following and are only referred from
69 ±8 percent of the time, showing a tendency to make, but
not an established policy of making, such references.

The policies suggested by this part of the study are
not intended to be absolute, but rather would consist of a
statement that such references would be made unless there
were a reason not to do so. It would be preferable to have
a few unneeded references in the catalog rather than to omit
significant numbers of useful ones. Such policies, which
could be extended to other types of headings, could cut down
on the number of decisions required of the cataloger by permitting him to make an important group of references more
or less automatically.

Implications of the Study and Suggestions for Further Research

Need for a subject heading code

The problems caused by the lack of a formal subject heading code, and the extreme need for, at a minimum, rationalization of subject headings, have been evident throughout this study. Inconsistencies in heading of formation and arrangement, lack of useful cross references and existence of unneeded ones, the variation in actual practice from what is thought to be practiced, all could be eliminated or at least reduced in magnitude by a formal code. Further research into other aspects of subject heading structure would contribute to a code. For instance, there were numerous indications throughout this study that many of the subject headings which cause problems are leftovers from earlier editions of the list which have never been changed to keep up with changes in the language. The large number of hyphenated words, discussed in Chapter VI, is an example. There were numerous other occasions where one or more headings which appeared anomalous in some way were checked and found to be carry-overs from the first edition of the LC subject headings. A formal study, analogous to Frarey's study of revision of LC headings in the decade 1941-1950, but extending from the first to the most recent editions of the heading list, would certainly be worthwhile.

Application of computer techniques to the problems of cataloging is hindered by the existing inconsistency and unpredictability found in subject headings. On the other side, as is discussed below, the availability of the computer makes possible types of studies which could not be considered in the past.

Faceting in the LC subject headings

      No formal evidence was collected on this point, but
it appears that the LC subject headings may be the best example of an informal faceted classification scheme in existence. "Informal" is, however, the operative word in this
case. To the author's knowledge it has never been suggested
in print that subject headings do have faceted aspects.
"Facets" may be defined as "terms denoting similar kinds
of concept."[1] Depending on the subject, applicable facets
might be materials, processes, places, parts of a unit,
forms of publication, operations performed on a thing, and
so on.

      The faceting in LC subject headings is flexible, and
sometimes inconsistent, apparently applied only when a need
is evident. It is based to a large extent on sub-arrangement by means of punctuation marks. Three useful examples
are the headings beginning Art, Cookery, and Negroes. The
sequence of headings in these groupings are summarized
below.

    Art (the term unmodified)
      Aspects and form subdivisions, set off by the dash.
      In specific places, set off by the dash.
      Of specific schools, types, cultures and (cross
        references only) such headings as Art, Effect of
        See Art therapy, treated as inversions using the
        comma.
      Of specific nationalities and ethnic groups, treated
        as inversions using the comma.
      Phrase headings beginning with Art, and including
        two subgroups in their appropriate alphabetical
        position: Art in relation to other subjects, all
        beginning Art and...; treatment of Art in other
        areas, beginning Art in...

    Cookery (unsubdivided heading)
      Aspects and form subdivisions, set off by the dash.
      By type of food, set off by parentheses.

Special types, treated as inversions.
Special places, ethnic, and cultural groups,
   treated as inversions.
Phrase headings, including Cookery for... [special
   groups].

Negroes (general works on Negroes in the United States)
   Aspects and form subdivisions, set off by the dash.
   In specific states or localities in the U.S., set off
      by the dash.
   Phrase headings, including:
      Negroes as... [part of other special groups,
         e.g., businessmen].
      Negroes in... [treatment in literature, etc.;
         in certain professional areas, such as medicine].
      Negroes in... [places other than the U.S.].

One thing that is immediately evident from the examples given above is that all the facets are not formally
identified and sub-arranged. Form subdivisions are not
separated from aspects; numerous types of aspects representing different facets are interfiled. Furthermore, faceting
in the LC list is ad hoc, a particular facet usually being
given separate treatment only when it includes a large number of headings. Equivalent facets are not treated in the
same way. In the examples above, Art which is physically
located in a given place receives the place name as a subdivision; Art produced by artists of a nation or group receives the name as an inversion. On the other hand, Negroes
(physically located) in specific parts of the United States receive the place name as subdivision, while Negroes (physically located) in other countries are entered under Negroes
in... [place].

Further research into the extent and nature of sub-
arrangement of subjects by facets, both in the LC list and in
the LC official catalog (where arrangement differs), should
make possible a formal specification of when facets are to

be used, and a procedure for making them explicit rather
than implicit as they are now.

<u>Other classificatory aspects of subject headings</u>

Aside from the fact that any ordering is by its nature
a form of classification, and that arrangement in the order
of the letters of the alphabet is therefore an arrangement by
classes, there are numerous other features of subject headings which involve a form of classification. The headings
for forms of music and instrument groupings required for
particular works, discussed in Chapter V, act as a classification alternate to the order provided by the shelf classification scheme at LC. In fact, all headings used to designate form or type of material, rather than actual subjects,
are classificatory in nature.

It would seem highly probable that the extensive
specification of legal headings in the LC list arises at least
partly as a substitute for schedule K (law) of the LC classification, only a single section of which has ever been
published, and that only within the past few years.

Numerous subject subdivisions represent a form of
classification. Perhaps the best example is the period subdivisions used with many headings and subdivisions, but
particularly with such subdivisions as <u>History</u> and <u>Politics
and government.</u> 'Period subdivision... [in history] should
either correspond to generally recognized epochs in the
history of the place or should represent spans of time frequently treated in books, whether they possess historic unity
or not. "[2] Many books are written about periods of time
which do not correspond to a period subdivision; in this case
the subdivision(s) most appropriate are used. A new subdivision corresponding precisely to the scope of the book is
not devised.

The practice of indirect geographical subdivision of subjects also represents a form of classification. This practice is, however, gradually being dispensed with.[3] An analysis, as suggested above, of changes in the LC list since its first edition might show further evidence of classification in subdivisions if, for instance, broader subdivisions in earlier editions were broken into several narrower ones in later years. This might be expected also on the ground of the results shown in Chapter II, that one reason for introduction of aspect subdivision is to break up long files.

Coordinate and complex subjects

There are numerous complex topics of which it is not possible to state with certainly that one part of the topic represents the subject, and the other part the aspect or point of view from which it is treated. One major example is the problem of which should be the entry point when a subject is treated in relation to a particular place. This question dates at least from Cutter's time, and has never been adequately resolved. The usages adopted in particular cases have generally been based on ad hoc decisions, but there is a semantic question involved: in what does a "place" consist? For example, it is certainly true that a book about the history of a place has as its subject the place, from the point of view of the place's history. On the other hand, a book about oil well drilling which draws most of its examples from that activity as carried on in a particular place is nevertheless a book about drilling oil wells. This is <u>not</u> to say that in actual practice, access by the aspect in the first instance, and by the place in the second, would not be useful. There are two points to be made. First, the place versus topic problem would appear

to be a continuum with a large gray area in the middle
where the response as to which is the actual subject will
depend largely on what, for a given person, is included in
the concept of "place" or "locality." Second, a theoretical
basis for subject headings is urgently needed, and this place
versus topic question is one area where theory is almost
totally lacking.

In other cases, the subject-aspect order may not
necessarily be the most useful one for the catalog even if
it is clear which part is subject and which is aspect. Some
practices which probably indicate a judgment on the usefulness of possible access points were found. Catalysis of or
by a substance may be regarded as a point of view from
which the substance as subject is treated. Practice in the
LC official catalog is to enter works about catalysis under
the heading Catalysis without modification, and also to enter
those works on specific substances or groups of substances
under the name of the substance without modification. The
result is a file of several hundred undifferentiated entries
under Catalysis, with no means of going directly to works
on catalysis involving special substances. While this practice surely represents a failure to subdivide a file which
needed it, it brings up the other point of just what is the
subject. There is no question about the subject of a work
on catalysis in general, or about the subject of a work on
all aspects of a particular compound. But a book about
catalysis of (for example) iron may be regarded as treating
of the subject iron from the point of view of catalyzation of
it, or as treating of a special kind of catalysis: that of iron.
The problem of specificity

        As discussed in Chapter I, the concept of specificity

has never been adequately defined. It is partly due to this
lack of definition that so many questions arise about desirable "limits" to specificity. This does not apply only to
the question of specificity of subject versus specificity of
subject and aspect. For instance, Lyric poetry is certainly
not an aspect of the general subject poetry; it is a special
kind. With somewhat less confidence it may be said that
poetry which happens to be written in the English language
is also a special kind of poetry. In this case there is no
justification under the principle of specific entry for the
scope note in the LC list under Lyric poetry stating that
general works only are entered under this heading, and that
works on the lyric poetry of a specific country are entered
under such headings as English poetry. The theories of
facet analysis could be of considerable value in attacking
these problems. There are parts of concepts other than the
subject itself and the point of view from which it is treated,
and the attempt to fit all the parts of a concept into these
two categories has its Procrustean aspects. This is not to
propose formal faceting in subject headings, but rather that
analysis of headings from the point of view of the facets
represented could make important contributions to understanding of the problems involved.

Need for access points other than subjects

     At several points throughout the report of this study,
headings which are not subject headings, but provide other
forms of access, have been mentioned or discussed at
length. As was pointed out in Chapters IV and V, these
other types of headings certainly provide much-needed access points. These other types include form and class
headings, and headings applied to special types of material.

The failure to distinguish them from subject headings makes it almost unavoidable that their application is inconsistent and does not represent a consciously thought-out policy. Research into appropriate uses of these headings is much needed.

The computer as an aid to subject heading research

Several parts of this study would not have been feasible without use of computer techniques. Now that the LC list is available in machine-readable form, many other aspects of structure and form are, for the first time, open to analysis. It will be possible to actually determine the structural characteristics of subject headings on a much larger scale than in the past. It should be observed that the feasibility of application of computer techniques to this area at present is limited not by the availability of knowledge of computing, but rather by the depth of knowledge required of subject heading structure.

Summary

The study reported here has proved fruitful in three major respects: (1) it has provided some factual support for the validity of a number of assumptions generally held regarding various aspects of subject heading structure and use; (2) it has provided some factual evidence in support of other, not previously formulated, assumptions; and (3) it has demonstrated the feasibility and usefulness of computer techniques for conducting analyses of subject heading structure.

Notes

1. John R. Sharp, <u>Some Fundamentals of Information Retrieval</u>, p. 33.

2. Haykin, <u>Subject Headings</u>, p. 33.

3. <u>Ibid.</u>, p. 32.

Appendix I

Selection, Keying, and Formatting
of the Main Sample

Sample selection

When selection of samples for testing the hypothesis was begun, it was known that the magnetic tape used by the Government Printing Office for computer composition of the seventh edition of the LC subject headings would be available at some time in the near future. Had it been available at that time, sample selection could have been much simpler and more economical. Since the tape was not then available, it seemed much wiser to select at least part of the samples by manual methods so that work would not be delayed.

Given the size of the universe--1,432 pages, containing about 100 headings and subdivisions per page--selection of individual headings for the sample would not have been feasible. In addition, some of the aspects of headings to be investigated were closely concerned with the arrangement of complex series of entries beginning with the same word. For these reasons the following procedure was used for selection of the sample.

From a random number table, 143 numbers in the range from one to 1,432 were selected. Numbers were then used to designate the page numbers of the LC list from which headings were to be punched. Since arrangement of complex series of heddings was important to the study, and

since headings and their subdivisions often run over from
one page to another, it was decided not to keypunch starting
from the first line on the page selected and ending at the
last line. If the first word of the last heading on the page
selected occurred as the first word in new headings on the
following page, these headings were also punched. Thus,
from some pages which contained only subdivisions of a
heading which began on a preceding page, or on which all
headings began with the same word as the last heading on
the page preceding, no headings at all were keypunched.
Conversely, where the subdivisions of a heading ran over
several pages, or the same first word was used in headings
following, all the headings on several pages were keypunched.

Of the printed material on a page or section of a
page in the sample, all the headings, subdivisions of all
levels, and see references were keypunched. If a suggested
LC classification number, instruction for direct or indirect
geographical subdivision, or both, were present, these were
keypunched also. The sa's (see also's), x's and xx's (reverse cross references) and scope and other notes were not
keypunched. Aside from limitations in resources and time,
it was not necessary to have this material in machine-
readable form in order to investigate the problems involved
in this study. On the ground of future utility of the machine-
readable data, the decision might have been different if it
had not been known that the entire LC list would (eventually)
be available on magnetic tape.

Keying procedure

The keypunching system was devised to require a
minimum of both editorial and punching effort, but simultaneously to make all required information accessible by

programming. The keypuncher keyed the data exactly as it
appeared in the list. Since each level of subdivision is
represented by a level of indentation in the printed list,
main headings were punched beginning in column one of the
card, subdivisions with a dash beginning in column two,
sub-subdivisions with a dash beginning in column three, and
so on. To improve keypuncher accuracy, lines were drawn
with a ruler at each level of indentation. Since the indentation for "See" instructions is not the same as that for
subdivisions after the first level, the instructions for these
were left flexible: the keypuncher could begin with the
word "See" anywhere from column two on.

The headings were keyed in all upper case; dia-
criticals and accents were omitted. All punctuation marks
(except the hyphen) were preceded or followed by a single
space, as appropriate, except that parentheses beginning a
sequence of characters in italics (i.e., instructions for
geographical subdivisions, or class number) were preceded
by two spaces.

Code numbers, described in Chapter VI on subject
heading styling, were written after those headings for which
they were required. The puncher keyed the heading in the
standard fashion, then two slashes, immediately followed by
the code numbers. Advantage was taken of this practice to
code an F after all headings which might be form headings
for that part of the study. A separate listing of such headings was then produced as a by-product of the styling program.

These keying conventions were explicit and simple
enough to be applied with minimal error by two different
keypunchers after a brief learning period. In fact, proof-

reading was required primarily for typographical errors, not for misapplication of the keying conventions.

Expansion to full subject headings

Although the same raw data, keyed as described above, were used in all three of the programs for heading analysis, the same general program element was used in all cases to expand subdivisions to full headings. This element used the keying conventions to determine if a given card was a heading, a subdivision of any level, or a see reference. The sequence below represents first the form in which headings were punched, and then the form to which these headings were expanded by the program element. Each line represents a single punched card.

It is clear that this processing step saved an enormous amount of keying; furthermore, it would not have been feasible to expect the keypuncher to perform this expansion accurately.

This sample was used for the entire study, with the exception of the comparison of Wilson and LC subject heading practice described in Chapter IV and the study of aspect subdivisions described in Chapter II. The ways in which it was processed for different purposes are described in the appropriate chapters.

Keypunching format

Mexico
  - Boundaries
    - U. S.
  - Constitutional law
  - Frontier troubles
    - To 1910 (F1234, New Southwest, F786, Texas, F391)
    - 1910- (F1234, New Southwest, F786, Texas, F391)

- History (F1203-1409)
  - To 1810
  - To 1519
  - Conquest, 1519-1540
    - Juvenile literature
    - Naval operations
      - Juvenile literature
  - Spanish colony, 1540-1810
  - 1810-
  - Wars of Independence, 1810-1821
  - 1821-1861
  - War with the U. S., 1845-1848
    See U. S. - History - War with Mexico, 1845-1848
  - European intervention, 1861-1867
  - 1867-1910
  - 1910-1946
  - 1946-
  - Presidents

Full headings, expanded by computer program

Mexico
Mexico - Boundaries
Mexico - Boundaries - U. S.
Mexico - Constitutional law
Mexico - Frontier troubles
Mexico - Frontier troubles - To 1910   (F1234, New Southwest, F786, Texas, F391)
Mexico - Frontier troubles - 1910- (F1234, New Southwest, F786, Texas, F391)
Mexico - History   (F1203-1409)
Mexico - History - To 1810
Mexico - History - To 1519
Mexico - History - Conquest, 1519-1540
Mexico - History - Conquest, 1519-1540 - Juvenile literature
Mexico - History - Conquest, 1519-1540 - Naval operations
Mexico - History - Conquest, 1519-1540 - Naval operations - Juvenile literature
Mexico - History - Spanish colony, 1540-1810
Mexico - History - 1810-
Mexico - History - Wars of Independence, 1810-1821
Mexico - History - 1821-1861
Mexico - History - War with the U. S., 1845-1848   See U. S. - History - War with Mexico, 1845-1848
Mexico - History - European intervention, 1861-1867
Mexico - History - 1867-1910

Mexico - History - 1910-1946
Mexico - History - 1946-
Mexico - Presidents

Appendix II

Program for Analysis of Subject
Heading Structure

This program produced the data for several parts of the study--particularly the sections on subdivisions, inversions, and cross references. The headings, keyed and expanded into their full forms as described in Appendix I, were then analyzed for the following structural characteristics:

1. Subdivisions of all levels.
2. Parenthetical expressions.
3. Inversions.
4. Series.
5. Prepositions, conjunctions and connectives.
6. Direct or indirect geographical subdivision.

Each time one of the above was found, the heading was inverted to bring the element involved to the beginning. The item was then appropriately labeled and punched out. If several of the structural elements were present, all were identified. Each element of a series was brought forward in turn. Furthermore, it was possible to distinguish inversions from series accurately in nearly all cases, even though the physical form, i.e., number of commas, was often identical.

In the very few cases (perhaps a few dozen in the entire sample) which were not analyzed correctly by the program, the cards were edited manually. They were then machine-sorted, producing a listing of all the terms which appeared in each kind of element. This listing permitted comparison of, for instance, the terms which were used as subdivisions with those used as inversions or in prepositional phrases.

The program also produced a listing of all see references as a by-product.

Appendix III

Program to List all Words Appearing
in Subject Headings

This program was used to provide additional insights into several questions which arose in the course of the study, but particularly the problem of selection of the prime entry term for a heading. It is quite simple: each word in a heading is brought forward, followed by the remainder of the heading, and then that part of the heading which preceded the word. The only exception was the conjunctions, prepositions, and connectives which were brought out by the program described in Appendix II.

Appendix IV

Glossary

In this study at various points the use of technical terms has been necessary.   Thos which represent
specialized definitions are included in the glossary below.
Such terms as "concept," "function," "principle," "sort,"
"system" and "theory" are used in their basic dictionary
sense.   The sources used are listed at the end of the
glossary; the source of any definitions not the work of the
author is shown in parentheses.

Definitions

Access point -- the first word of an entry; in this
    study, the first word of a subject heading.

Alphabetico-classed subject catalog -- An alphabetical subject
    catalog, in which the entry words of the heading consist
    of selected generic subjects.   Under each generic entry
    word, its included specific topics are cited as subhead-
    ings, and sub-arranged alphabetically.   The stepping
    down process for citing more restricted subjects may
    be carried to further stages (Coates).

Alphabetico-specific -- A subject catalog in which the alpha-
    betically arranged headings state precisely the subject
    of each document... or other literary unit chosen as the
    basis for indexing.   The subject part of a dictionary
    catalog constructed on the specific entry principle is
    included in this definition (Coates).

Aspect -- Point of view from which a subject may be treated.

Chain   -- A hierarchy of terms in a classification scheme,

each term containing or including all those which follow it (Coates).

Chain indexing -- A semi-mechanical method of producing the requisite subject index entries for a classified catalog, based on analysis of the classification symbol for each subject [usually using in succession the terms represented by each part of the classification symbol] (Landau).

Coordinate indexing -- A method of indexing by the joint use of two or more terms, so that retrieval is performed by the logical operations of product, sum, and complement...[among two or more terms] (Taylor).

Facet -- A particular aspect of a subject..., e.g., in literature may be seen four facets--language, form, author, work (Landau).

Facet analysis -- The enumeration of the possible trains of characteristics [q.v.] by which a main class can be divided (Ranganathan, cited by Vickery).

Post-coordinate system -- A system of subject analysis in which only documents satisfying some condition of presence or absence of more than one index term are selected for retrieval.

Pre-coordinate system -- A system of subject analysis in which index terms assigned may be complex, and typically, documents are retrieved on the basis of the presence or absence of a single term.

Term -- Any form of class, subclass, subject heading, single word, or combination of words assigned to an item of information so as to characterize it (Jonker).

Train of characteristics -- A succession of characteristics used in subdividing a universe so as to yield in succession wholes and not leading to organs or constituents (Ranganathan, cited by Vickery).

Sources of definitions

E. J. Coates. Subject Catalogs: Headings and Structure
      London: The Library Association, 1960. p. 9-13.

Frederick Jonker. Indexing Theory, Indexing Methods, and
    Search Devices. New York: Scarecrow Press,
    1964. p. 20.

Thomas Landau, ed. Encyclopedia of Librarianship.
    London: Bowes and Bowes, 1958.

Robert S. Taylor, comp. Glossary of Terms Frequently
    used in Scientific Documentation. New York:
    American Institute of Physics, 1962.

Brian C. Vickery. "Glossary of Current Terminology."
    Depth Classification and Reference Service and
    Reference Materials. Edited by S. R. Ranganathan.
    Delhi: Indian Library Association, 1953. p. 27-46.

Bibliography

American Library Association. ALA Rules for Filing Cata-
    log Cards. Chicago: American Library Association,
    1942.

_____. ALA Rules for Filing Catalog Cards. 2nd ed.
    Chicago: American Library Association, 1968.

Brinkler, Bartol. "Geographical Approach to Materials in
    the Library of Congress Subject Headings." Library
    Resources and Technical Services, VI (Winter, 1962),
    49-64.

Brooks, Benedict and Kilgour, Frederick G. "Comparison
    of Library of Congress Subject Headings and Medical
    Subject Headings." Medical Library Association
    Bulletin, LII (April, 1964), 414-419.

Coen, James A. "An Investigation of Indirect Subdivision by
    Place in Library of Congress Subject Headings."
    Library Resources and Technical Services, XIII
    (Winter, 1969), 60-76.

Cronin, John W. "The National Union and Library of Con-
    gress Catalogs: Problems and Prospects." Library
    Quarterly, XXXIV (January, 1964), 77-96.

Cutter, Charles A. Rules for a Printed Dictionary Cata-
    logue. Washington: Gov't. Printing Office, 1876.

_____. Rules for a Dictionary Catalog. 4th ed. London:
    Library Association, 1953.

Daily, Jay E. "The Grammar of Subject Headings; A Form-
    ulation of Rules for Subject Headings based on a
    Syntactical and Morphological Analysis of the Library
    of Congress List." Unpublished D. L. S. dissertation,
    Columbia University, 1957.

_____. "Many Changes, No Alteration." Library Journal,
XCII (November 1, 1967), 3961-3963.

Darling, Louise. "Readers' Impressions of the Subject
Catalog." Medical Library Association Bulletin,
XLIX (January, 1961), 58-62.

Field, Oliver T. "An Application of the Direct Entry Principle to Indexing." American Documentation, VII
(July, 1956), 225-228.

Frarey, Carlyle J. "Subject Heading Revision by the Li-
brary of Congress, 1941-1950." Unpublished
Master's essay, School of Library Service, Columbia
University, 1951.

_____. Subject Headings. State of the Library Art, Vol. I,
Part 2. New Brunswick, N.J.: Rutgers University
Press, 1960.

Haydock, Eleanor. "MeSH List and Book Cataloging in
Medical Libraries." Medical Library Association
Bulletin, LII (July, 1964), 545-556.

Haykin, David J. "Project for a Subject Heading Code,"
Rev. Sept., 1957 (Mimeographed)

_____. Subject Headings: A Practical Guide. Washington:
Gov't. Printing Office, 1951.

Hines, Theodore C. and Harris, Jessica L. Computer
Filing of Index, Bibliographic, and Catalog Entries.
Newark, N.J.: Bro-Dart Foundation, 1966.

Jackson, Sidney L. "Sears and Library of Congress Subject
Headings, Report of a Sample Comparison." Illinois
Libraries, XLIV (November, 1962), 608-630.

Kaiser, J. Systematic Indexing. London: Pitman, 1911.

Knapp, Patricia B. "Subject Catalog in the College Library:
an Investigation of Terminology." Library Quarterly,
XIV (July, 1944), 214-228.

Kučera, Henry and Francis, W. Nelson. Computational
Analysis of Present-Day American English. Provi-
dence, R.I.: Brown University Press, 1967.

Lilley, Oliver L. "Evaluation of the Subject Catalog: Criticisms and a Proposal." American Documentation, V (April, 1954), 41-60.

_____. "How Specific is 'Specific?' " Journal of Cataloging and Classification, XI (January, 1955), 3-8.

_____. "Terminology, Form, Specificity and the Syndetic Structure of Subject Headings for English Literature." Unpublished D. L. S. dissertation, Columbia University, 1959.

Mann, Margaret. Introduction to Cataloging and the Classification of Books. 2nd ed. Chicago: American Library Association, 1943.

Metcalfe, John W. Information Indexing and Subject Cataloging. New York: Scarecrow, 1957.

_____. Subject Classifying and Indexing of Libraries and Literature. New York: Scarecrow, 1959.

_____. Alphabetical Subject Indication of Information. Rutgers Series on Systems for the Intellectual Organization of Information, Vol. III. New Brunswick, N. J.: Graduate School of Library Service, Rutgers University, 1965.

Nugent, William R. "The Mechanization of the Filing Rules for the Dictionary Catalogs of the Library of Congress." Library Resources and Technical Services, XI (Spring, 1967), 145-166.

Osborn, Andrew D. The Crisis in Cataloging. New York: American Library Institute, 1941.

Pettee, Julia. Subject Headings; the History and Theory of the Alphabetical Subject Approach to Books. New York: H. W. Wilson, 1947.

Prévost, Marie-Louise. "An Approach to Theory and Method in General Subject Heading." Library Quarterly, XVI (April, 1946), 140-151.

Rogers, Frank B. "Problems of Medical Subject Cataloging." Bulletin of the Medical Library Association, LVI (October, 1968), 355-364.

Roth, Harold L., Hines, Theodore C. and Colverd, Martin.
Technical Services for the Memphis and Shelby
County Public Libraries; Report of a Study made for
the Libraries. East Orange, N.J.: Rothines Asso-
ciates, 1967.

Rue, Eloise and LaPlante, Effie. Subject Headings for
Children's Materials. Chicago: American Library
Association, 1952.

Sears, Minnie E. List of Subject Headings. 9th ed. Edited
by Barbara M. Westby. New York: H. W. Wilson,
1965.

Sewell, Winifred. "Medical Subject Headings in MEDLARS."
Medical Library Association Bulletin, LII (January,
1964), 164-170.

Sharp, Henry A. "Cataloguing: Some New Approaches. 5.
The Dictionary Subject Approach." Library World,
LVII (December, 1955), 92-94.

Sharp, John R. Some Fundamentals of Information Retrieval. New York: London House & Maxwell, 1965.

Tauber, Maurice, ed. Subject Analysis of Library Materials.
New York: Columbia University, 1953.

_____., et al. Technical Services in Libraries. New York:
Columbia University Press, 1954.

U.S. Library of Congress. Filing Rules for the Dictionary
Catalogs of the Library of Congress. Washington:
Gov't. Printing Office, 1956.

_____. Subject Headings used in the Dictionary Catalogs of
the Library of Congress. 6th ed. Edited by
Marguerite V. Quattlebaum. Washington: Library
of Congress, 1957.

_____. Subject Headings used in the Dictionary Catalogs of
the Library of Congress. 7th ed. Edited by
Marguerite V. Quattlebaum. Washington: Library
of Congress, 1966.

U.S. National Library of Medicine. "Medical Subject Headings." Index Medicus, VI (January, 1965).

Van Hoesen, H. B.   "Perspective in Cataloging with some
    Applications." Library Quarterly, XIV (April, 1944),
    100-107.

Vatican Library.   Norme per il Catalogo degli Stampati.
    Citta del Vaticano: Biblioteca Apostolica Vaticana,
    1931.

_____. Règles pour le catalogue des imprimés.   Edition
    Française (Texte établi sur la troisième edition
    italienne).   Cité du Vatican: Bibliothèque
    Apostolique Vaticane, 1950.

_____. Rules for the Catalog of Printed Books.   Translated
    from the 2nd Italian edition by T. J. Shanahan,
    et al.   Edited by W. E. Wright.   Chicago: American
    Library Association, 1948.

Weaver, Warren.   "Recent Contributions to the Mathematical
    Theory of Communication." The Mathematical Theory
    of Communication.   Edited by Claude E. Shannon and
    Warren Weaver.   Urbana, Ill.: University of
    Illinois Press, 1964.

This index was produced on the computer from human-generated entries using programs written by Dr. Theodore Hines and the author. The programs are part of an experimental set written for research in unit operations in information handling and for student use at Columbia University School of Library Service. The design used provides great flexibility, especially in formatting. As these programs are still highly experimental, comments on the format and other features of the index would be most welcome. As with all the programs in the set, there was no limit on field length, and coding was limited to the sort that would be used in normal typing.

Grateful acknowledgments are due to Grolier, Inc. and Bro-Dart Industries, who partially supported the development of the program, and to the Columbia University Computer Center and its Director, Dr. Kenneth King, for their wholehearted support of this and other research activities.

J. L. H.

INDEX

ASPECT SUBDIVISIONS (CONT'D)   257

Aspect subdivisions (cont'd)
  use of   47-60
    and file length   39, 52-58, 221
    as accident of phraseology   52
    distribution with particular headings   53-58
    factors in   40
    Haykin on   47-48
    limited by needs   26
Atlases
  Haykin on headings for   113

Author entries
 SEE ALSO Corporate names
 SEE ALSO Geographical names
  arrangement under Hines-Harris code   164-165
B. C. dates
  computer filing program provision for   195
Bibliographic control
  aided by subject access   38
Biographies
  treatment of collections in Sears list   114
Book titles
 SEE Titles
Brinkler, Bartol
  on correlation of LC class and choice between
    place and subject entry   36-37
Bro-Dart
 SEE Alanar
Brooks, Benedict
  study comparing LC headings and MeSH   29-30
Card density per inch
  in LC catalogs   125
Cataloger's choice headings
  being abandoned by LC   36
Catalogs
  computer produced   41
Catchword title catalog
  use in Germany   15
Catchword title entry
  defined   44
  LC use of   25
Catchword title indexing
  influence on subject heading development   14
Century Dictionary
  use as spelling authority in LC subject headings
                                                  161
Chain indexing
  in subject headings   19
Children's collections
  subject headings for   93
Class, conceptual distinction
  from aspect   85
  from kind   89